First time M̶o̶m̶s̶

PRIOR TO PREGNANCY.

LESS FEAR MORE CHEER

Book 1

Sarah S Keller

© 2019

COPYRIGHT

TABLE OF CONTENTS

*****

PART ONE

PREPPING YOUR BODY

*****

CHAPTER ONE: SUPPLEMENTS—YOUR

PRENATAL

I'm sure you've sat down and thought out everything about your pregnancy, your baby's birth, how much you'll love and coddle your newborn, and about your wonderful life together! You probably know if you have more of a chance of having a boy or girl, if you want twins or even triplets, and what name you want for each gender. I'm sure you've picked out the nursery colors, the theme, and the furniture design. Let me guess... Arnold Schwarzenegger, right? Just kidding! Don't kill me yet!

My husband and I picked out our first son's name ten years before he was born—before we were even intimate! We were engaged and awaiting our wedding date, when, sitting at work one day, bored out of my mind, I started brainstorming. *"When we marry, if God gives us kiddos, what will their names be?"*

I made two columns, one entitled "girl" and one entitled "boy." It irked me that the dividing line wasn't straight, so I threw that piece of paper away and, using another piece of paper as a ruler, drew myself a perfectly straight line. Yes, I have an OCD diagnosis. I listed several names for girls and circled the ones that stuck out to me, then highlighted the ones that you didn't hear very often.

As I said, I was bored. I worked in a nursery. It was clean, and all my kids had gone home.

I rewrote my list, mark-free.

I didn't end up with as many names on the boy's side. I couldn't really think of many boy names that weren't popular. Finally, I was hit alongside the head with a brilliant idea! Matthew's middle name was Samuel. Why not name our first boy Samuel? Matt had already told me he didn't want any Juniors, but this... this was a home run!

When I *finally* got off work that afternoon, I met Matt at our usual spot, the college snack-shop. I presented my list. He loved the idea of Samuel's name.

Ten years later, we had our first boy and dubbed him Samuel Isaiah. He is such a little mischief maker—such a card!

If you and your one and only are thinking of making a little life, there are some things you must do before beginning your quest! Prepping your body is very important. There are some things you should start, like a good exercise program and good vitamins, things you should stop, like smoking and full-on alcohol consumption, and things you should maintain, like a healthy diet. Let's break it down.

****SUPPLEMENTS****

I remember trying to choke down my first supplement. It was horrible! It was the size of a horse pill and the color of yesterday's leftover pancakes, which I'd eaten around the lump in my throat, by the way, just because Matt had made them for me. The vitamin smelled like... I don't know what it smelled like. Chemicals? A dirty sock mixed with a parakeet's cage? *Oh, the joy of 2005! They've come so far with taste and smell since then!* I put it in my mouth and tried to swallow it. I tried hard. I took a gulp of water. I tilted my head back and tried again. It all came back out... right along with my prenatal vitamin that I'd paid an arm and a leg for. Now, here I was, hemiplegic, and nothing to show for it! No, I hadn't started my prenatals when I began readying my body for conception—when I started prepping my body. No one had ever told me to. No one had ever told me a lot of things. I'm so glad prenatal vitamins have changed so much for your sake, but I envy you. I know the cheap vitamins still taste nasty, but I envy your ability to pay a little more to take prenatal vitamins without gagging. And, I envy your ability to read this book with all its advice.

Several supplements are important to us women of childbearing age. There are conception-aiding supplements all over Amazon that claim to help in ovulation and fertility. We should, more importantly, be choking down Prenatals and other vitamins and minerals. Some of these crucial vitamins and minerals can be supplied through food, while others can be fully obtained only through supplements!

THE WHYS

You may be asking, like me, "Are those nasty tasting prenatal vitamins *really* necessary?" I mean, they're so big and so horrible and so... Yes. Unfortunately, they are. I spent fifteen years choking them down, and trust me, when morning sickness hits you about two weeks to a month after conception, it's even harder to swallow them, so get as many nutrients in now as you can.

Making sure your baby-body-to-be has all the proper nourishment it needs to be able to conceive and carry your baby is vital. Even if you make a steady, balanced diet of all the healthiest foods you can think of, you still need to supplement. Food itself can't cover all of the bases.

There are times when taking a prenatal becomes more important yet. These include those of us who may have the following health issues, dietary restrictions, or complications:

- **Those with Certain Blood Disorders**— Several blood cell disorders can be affected by vitamins. A blood cell disorder is where there's a problem with the blood cells or platelets, not allowing them to function or form correctly.

  Anemia is one of these. There are several types of anemia. Anemia requires an iron supplement to correct it. Pernicious anemia, which keeps your body from taking what you need from the food you eat, is corrected with shots of B_{12}. B_9 is also used. Another name for B_9 is folate. B_{12} is dubbed cobalamin.

- **Those with Chronic Diseases**—Americans who are overweight and obese account for 70% of the adult population. Of the 857,460 people who died in 2017 just from diabetes, heart disease, and from stroke, only three of the many Chronic Diseases, obesity and being overweight played a significant part.

  Doctors try to show this to their patients, but many just don't care. In fact, out of all the people who have had a physical this year and were warned about their weight, more than 75% of them ignored the doctor's advice.

  Sadly, of those asked, only 33% reported having received any information from their doctor about eating a healthy lifestyle at all. When the doctors were interviewed, many of them didn't even know enough about nutrition to teach their patients about it!

I know the only healthcare provider I ever had that told me how to eat was my OB nurse, Sandy. I will forever remember her name. She was my nurse through five of my six pregnancies—four beautiful children and two angel babies. Miss Sandy will always be my angel.

A few of the most common chronic diseases we, as women, face today are diabetes, depression, and high blood pressure. These are things we need to get under control before we start working toward our baby bump. The key to this is a good exercise program, proper nutrition (not that processed junk we all find ourselves eating these days), and taking our supplements to fill in the gaps.

- **Those Who Have Had Gastric Bypass Surgery**—Even if you eat the most nutritious food there is, even if you follow the most balanced diet you can, even if you spend hours on Google searching for the perfect foods to eat, you'll *always* need vitamins once you've had gastric bypass surgery. Your stomach was specially designed, by your surgeon, to not be able to absorb all the calories you eat anymore. Unfortunately, it can't absorb all the vitamins you eat either. Your body needs vitamin B_{12}, a multivitamin with iron, at least 1200 mg of Calcium (up to 500 mg at a time), and possibly some other vitamins as well. You'll have to speak to your doctor to see about a test to check if you're deficient in anything else. This is why taking a prenatal is so essential to your health and will be so crucial to your new baby's health as well.

- **Those with an Eating Disorder**—A few disorders are as follows: <u>Pica</u> is eating things that aren't meant for human consumption—think dirt and paint. <u>Anorexia nervosa</u> is seeing yourself as fat even though you weigh less, usually much less, than 85% of what you're supposed to weigh. Due to this, people with anorexia nervosa effectively starve themselves. <u>Compulsive overeating</u> is another disorder. This is not being able to stop eating even though you're full. The last disorder we'll discuss, bulimia, is eating like mad, then trying to make yourself vomit, use diuretics, laxatives, and/or enemas to *make* yourself "go," or going without food for a while to make up for it. You might also exercise excessively to burn off the calories you just ingested. Most people doing this are women (85-90% of people). When we do this, we don't get the vitamins and minerals out of the food. We simply gorge ourselves and empty ourselves like a trashcan (…at least the trashcans in my house get stuffed, pressed down, and overfilled before they're emptied. Can anyone else testify?). Each of these disorders can lead to malnutrition.

- **Those with Food Allergies**—I'm sure you're familiar with the subject of food allergies. Many people are. FARE (Food Allergy Research & Education) states that there are 15 million people in the U.S. with an allergy to any one (or several) of the 170 known foods that can cause allergic reactions. Your immune system responds to certain foods differently than the rest of ours. It identifies the specific protein in that food as the enemy and sends out the troops to take down the "enemy forces." This, of course, causes quite the scene between your antibodies and the "invading army." These food allergies, this war inside your body, can cause anything from digestive symptoms to skin reactions, and even lead up to death. Ninety percent of the food allergies can be accounted for in eight foods. These are eggs, tree nuts, peanuts, milk, shellfish, wheat, fish, and soybeans.

Food allergies should be treated with the strictest of rules and regulations whenever you *do* become pregnant. Stick

13

warning signs all over yourself, Sweetheart! DO NOT GO ANYWHERE NEAR THEM! Don't even tempt yourself. Read the labels on your packaged food carefully—it's best to do this while shopping. Don't worry; you'll get faster with practice. Have fresh or pre-cooked and frozen meals in the fridge ready to go at a moment's notice in case a craving for a taboo food hits. Get used to it now. If you don't, you'll not be prepared come baby-time. The problem with having to avoid these foods is that you are not getting the vitamins and minerals you and your baby-to-be need to thrive.

By the way, just to ease your mind, Dr. Dan Atkins, the Director of Ambulatory Pediatrics at National Jewish Medical and Research Center, said that "normally, an unborn baby will not be affected by food allergies unless the woman has a severe reaction." Is this case, he's speaking of complete body shut-down, which would slow the blood flow to your baby. So, as you can see, the presence of food allergies is *not* a reason to avoid having that bundle of joy.

- **Those with Food Intolerances**—Intolerances are even more prevalent in our society than food allergies. The difference between these and allergies is that food allergies involve your immune system, while food intolerances only affect your digestive system. Your stomach can do all sorts of weird things from it. There's the gas and bloating, cramping (which seems like it should go with the gas part anyway, right?), to diarrhea or constipation (*Can't they make up their mind*). It can also cause nausea, ranging from mild to extreme.

There are a few reasons for these intolerances to rear their ugly head. One is that your body might not be able to handle the food additives or preservatives that are used in the foods. These include things like MSG (Stay away from that Chinese food!), sulfites, or artificial colors (That's how my husband knew I snuck one of the kids' fruit roll-ups… *stupid blood sugar anyway*). It could be that your body doesn't have the enzymes it needs to digest the particular food you're trying to eat. It could be, thirdly, a sensitivity to chemicals, like caffeine. Lastly, broccoli, onions, Brussels sprouts, and more contain natural sugars (*sneaky foods*). You could have a sensitivity to these sugars.

One example of food intolerance might be lactose intolerance. This is an instance of your body not having those enzymes it needs. When forced to avoid lactose, you must seek out other forms of calcium and Vitamin D, which can be found in prenatals.

It also seems, according to "The Food Connection," that women have more food intolerances than men do. It seems we get stuck with it all! It's probably a good idea, since so many of us have food allergies, intolerances, and avoidances, to see a nutritionist about your diet to see what you might be lacking.

- **Those with Food Avoidances**— Many people avoid things on purpose, whether it be to lose weight, for their health, or for other reasons. For instance, I am on the Ketogenic Diet to help control my seizures. My father-in-law is on the Atkins Diet to lose weight. There are others, like vegetarians and vegans, who follow their diets as a way of life. Some people, like the Hindu, don't eat certain meat, like beef, for religious reasons.

The perfectly followed, correctly executed, balanced diet of the vegan is perfectly nutritious for every age and stage of life, but, when not followed correctly, the diet lacks in several areas. It's complicated to follow the vegan diet to a "T." It must be balanced and well-planned. If you don't meet all the exact requirements of the diet plus the laws of a balanced diet, you may be deficient in the long-chain omega-3 fatty acids EPA and DHA, vitamin B_{12}, calcium, iron, vitamin D, zinc, iodine, and riboflavin. You need all of these to keep yourself and your future baby happy and healthy. It's recommended to start prepping your body with these vitamins for at least a month before you start trying to get pregnant. Where can you find them all in one convenient spot, packaged up and tied with a bow? Yep! You guessed it—your prenatal.

THE WHEN

So, when do you take them? When is the best time? After all... aren't there side effects to combat? Would it be best to take it before bed? With food? Milk? Without? On an empty stomach? What do I do? Whoa! Slow down! Listen up! Let's get into that here!

There really is no right or wrong time to take a prenatal vitamin. There's no specific time of the day that it absorbs better into your body than others. The "best time" for you is just something **you** will have to experiment with to find what's best for **you**.

Some prenatals can make you feel queasy if you take them on an empty stomach. Try taking them with a meal if they do. Some make you nauseous regardless. In this case, take them with just a few saltines and, otherwise, on a mostly empty stomach.

The best time for me was simply when I could remember. I was sick ALL THE TIME *for the whole pregnancy up until around 7 months along* with my first so no matter when I took it, I usually came close to losing it or lost it anyway. I was a "bad mommy" and gave up on prenatals for a while... Heck! I gave up on food for a while too! The only thing I could eat for the first few months was mashed potatoes and cheddar cheese. I found out that it was perfectly fine. In fact, the doctor said not to force myself to eat, just to eat as I could.

With my second I was sick for the mandatory three months, but after that I was good. I set a schedule—every day with supper and took my prenatal vitamin daily. This schedule helped me remember to take it. Now, some days I forgot, but we'll blame that on pregnancy brain and leave that alone.

Here's what the experts say:

- *What is the best time of the day to take your prenatal?* "Whatever time of the day you'll best remember to take it."—Sharon Phelan, MD [https://www.thetoddle.com/best-time-day-take-prenatal-vitamins/]

- *What is the best time of the day to take your prenatal?* "Take it at the same time each day. For some women, taking it in the evening before bed is easier on their stomach. Try to take your prenatal vitamin every day. If you have morning sickness, take it when you don't feel nauseous and when you're not vomiting."—*Your Pregnancy Quick Guide*, Glade B. Curtis, Judith Schuler [https://www.thetoddle.com/best-time-day-take-prenatal-vitamins/]

WHICH ONE?

Choosing the right prenatal vitamin has to do with making sure it's slam-packed full of all the nutrients you need.

The Good	The Amount	The Why
Folic Acid (B₉)	400-600 mcg	It aids in the formation of your baby-to-be's neural tube.
Iodine	150 mcg	It helps with the brain development and thyroid development of your baby-to-be.
Iron	150 mg	It keeps you from becoming anemic and is, later, your baby's cell builder.
Vitamin B₆	2mg	It may help morning sickness be a little more sympathetic.

There are other vitamins on the label that should be considered as well--for the good, the bad, and the ugly... Below are a few of the other vitamins listed on the prenatal vitamins.

The Okay	The Amount	The Why	The Ugly
Calcium	NO MORE THAN 250 mg	It is crucial for growing those little bones of that future baby-to-be.	Calcium and Iron absorption just don't mix.
Copper	2 mg	It maintains bone, nerve, and immune system health as well as forming blood cells.	
Vitamin A	800 mcg or 4,000 IU	NOTE: It may be replaced with Beta Carotene on the label.	Getting over 10,000 IU can be toxic.
Vitamin C	50-80 mg	It helps your immune system to fight off viruses and assists in the	Combining this with other supplements to get over 2,000 mg can cause danger to

		absorption of iron.	your baby.
Vitamin D	600 IU	It takes vitamin D to help your body absorb Calcium, which helps yours and your future baby's bones grow stronger.	Most women are deficient in vitamin D. The doctor will screen for this at your prenatal checkup, which we'll discuss later.
Zinc	15 mg	This is a mineral rather than a vitamin. It supports healthy cell division for you and future "Sam Junior." It also helps your immune system.	

**If you happen to be on a restricted diet, make sure your physician or nutritionist knows about it so they can make sure you're getting all the vitamins and minerals your body will need to support you and your baby-to-be!

22

Other things you're going to want to consider is whether your prenatal gives you side effects you can't live with and whether or not you can swallow it without it getting stuck in your throat. Is it the right prenatal for you? I don't know. That's for **you** to decide, and you have however long you and your man decide to wait before you decide to start trying for that kiddo to figure it out. Good luck!

Chapter Two: Supplements—Your Prenatal and Folic Acid

"We **can't** go outside, Mommy!" Samuel exclaimed in fear.

"Why forever not?" I asked.

"Acid rain, Mommy! It's Acid rain!" He pointed his little finger out the window.

I leaned forward in curiosity to peer out. *What in the world was he talking about?* The front yard was full of thick fog. We had just watched a Christmas special of *Dr. Who* the night before that had to do with acid rain coming to burn up Christmas Land. *Yes, we watched Sci-Fi with our 4-year-old. No, there weren't any monsters. Yes, Christmas was saved, Yes, my husband had watched it beforehand to make sure it was kid-friendly. Now that I've spoiled your Dr. Who Christmas Special, let's move on.*

He was absolutely convinced that there was acid rain outside, that if we went out, we'd be melted, and that we should **not** leave the house for the doctor's appointment. I finally convinced him we'd be just fine and that God would take care of us, but fog was "acid rain" for the longest time!

FOLIC ACID

"Folic Acid in my stomach?"—Don't worry, it's not like Samuel's acid. Also known as vitamin B_9 and folate, this is a vitamin that you simply cannot get enough of in your food. Folic acid is an essential vitamin for anyone that is prepping their body for pregnancy, trying to conceive, or pregnant already. Most prenatal vitamins have plenty of folic acid in them to cover all the bases.

If you want to take full advantage of folic acid's benefits, which I know you do, you'll want to begin taking the recommended dose every day for at least a month before ovulation day. "How do I tell *ovulation day?*" Just wait. We'll get there.

DOSING

You should never take any more than 1,000 mcg of folic acid daily, especially if you're at risk of being B_{12} deficient. An overabundance of folic acid in your system would make it difficult to detect any B_{12} deficiency that is there. If you're a Vegan, you're at risk, so make sure you're checking the labels on your prenatal vitamins for your percentages.

You should always be careful of your intake, even if you're not at risk. Taking more than the recommended 400 mcg before conception and 600 mcg after can lead to problems. Some circumstances make it necessary to take more than the recommended dose. However, leave the dosing up to your provider!

Your physician might instruct you to begin taking more folic acid for one of four reasons, though there may be more. If you have a genetic variation, called methylenetetrahydrofolate reductase (MTHFR) mutation, which would make it hard for your body to absorb the folic acid you need, it'll be suggested you take extra. Having diabetes may necessitate more folic acid be administered. Carrying twins may carry with it the necessity to up your dose to 1,000 mcg. I have seizures. Taking certain seizure meds, like Dilantin, Tegretol and Tegretol XR, Carbatrol, and Dolantin, raise the chances of your bundle of joy being born with an NTD, causing your physician to up our dose of folic acid.

FOOD SOURCES

Okay, now you can ask about those foods. There are several sources of folic acid in foods today. You see, the U.S. Food and Drug Administration requires that cereal, bread, rice, and pasta manufacturers add it to their foods! There are other foods that folic acid must be added to as well. In fact, one serving of some of these new-fangled breakfast cereals is loaded down with the whole amount of folic acid you need for the day. All Bran, Cap'N Crunch, Mini Spooners, and Life are excellent choices.

My ten-year-old loves cereal. She loves to sit there and eat it, and eat it, and eat it, that is. "Well, I still had milk left over, so I **had** to add more cereal… Well, I still had cereal left, so I **had** to add more milk… Well, I still…" You get the idea. We've nipped that in the bud by the way! The manufacturers are not claiming that eating bowl upon bowl of cereal in one sitting gets you your daily requirement of folic acid, but that your daily value is met in one serving. This is usually anywhere between ¾ of a cup and 1 ½ cups depending on the cereal—just in case you were wondering.

This helps those who are not planning to become pregnant, but we don't eat the same cereal every single day or in the exact same amount, so we can't know the precise number of nutrients we're getting from it. The problem, when it comes to those of you trying to get pregnant, or those of you in the prepping stage, is that, even by measuring out the exact amount of cereal you need, all the goodies end up on the bottom of the bowl, meaning you didn't get all the folic acid anyway.

There are "real foods" that have folate (folic acid) in them, too, but they are not a good source either. The reasons for this should really be found on one of those shows, "Twelve of the Weirdest Things You've Never Heard Of," or something. Did you know (QUESTION #1) your body actually absorbs folic acid easier via supplement than it can via the natural folate from food? Here's another, (QUESTION #2) True or False: Folate can dissipate from the foods during the time it's in storage. (TRUE). Lastly, (QUESTION #3) what do you think about this statement? —Folate can be cooked out of the food in the preparation process. It's absolutely true!

"Should we even bother with the foods that are rich in folate if it's going to do nothing anyway?" I didn't say it wasn't going to do anything. Asking that question is like my daughter asking why she has to look over the dishes her sister washed before putting them away. *Um. Because if you don't, something might get missed.* If you eat food rich in folate along with your supplement (which is what your folic acid is meant to do—supplement an already implemented diet, or fill in the gaps where something might have been missed), then you have a better chance at a healthy you during pregnancy and a happy, healthy baby to hold at the end.

Foods rich in folate include:

- Dried peas, beans, and nuts

- Dark green vegetables, such as spinach, okra, asparagus, broccoli, turnip or collard greens, and Brussel sprouts

- Citrus juice and fruit

- Lentils

- Avocados

My oldest daughter, when she was about 3-years-old, decided she was *not* going to eat her peas. Her refusal turned into a normal thing for every vegetable. I wasn't sure what to do. I spoke to her doctor, who suggested I hide her veggies in something she liked. That evening, I made macaroni and cheese, chicken, and peas. Do you know where the peas went? Inside the macaroni and cheese. Guess what she ate that night? All her peas. If you can't down these folate-rich foods, hide them. Add them to things that you do like. Camouflage them. You can do it! Sierra and I both are cheering you on!

Here's another story. When my third, was about five, we had a hurricane come through. Afterward, we were driving down a back road toward "Grandma and Pop's house" when we blew through a stop sign. *I say "blew through", but we were only going 25 because we were in the back part of a subdivision.* We'd driven that way several times before, but Matt had forgotten about the sign since it happened to be lying on the ground. The next time we came through, it was back up. Rebekka was so excited to find that it was as short as she was that we *had* to stop and take a picture! Apparently, they had just cut it off where it had been bent in half by the wind and planted it again.

There are signs to watch for in your body that will tell you if you have a folic acid deficiency. They can be subtle, or they can be full-on up in your face:

- **Diarrhea**—We all know what diarrhea is. In our family, we just say, "I've got the poops," in case you were wondering. It causes, as we all know so well, cramps, a sore bottom, dehydration, and that annoying, constant running to the bathroom.

Besides medicines like Pepto-Bismol, which can be used to help with the frequency of the movements, there are also natural remedies that may benefit you. One of my friends from the Bahamas once suggested sipping a hot cup of water with lemon in it to take care of gas pains. It works!

Taking probiotics will help diarrhea lessen. In typical cases, it helps it to last one day less and decrease the length of your symptoms to four days max in 60% of diarrhea cases. You can also restore that "good bacteria" in your gut, like Bifidobacterium and Lactobacillus acidophilus, by eating yogurt.

Try eating ¼ to ½ of a cup of home-pureed carrots hourly. This will help since carrots are a source of pectin. Pectin has been used for years to control diarrhea.

Implement the BRAT diet. Eat bananas, rice, applesauce, and toast. One of the best things about the BRAT diet, when you have an upset GI tract, is that all these foods are bland and soothing. Besides that, the applesauce and bananas, both, contain that same wonderful fiber that carrots do—pectin.

- **Weakness**— To work correctly, muscle cells have to recognize the signals the brain sends its way and then signal the brain back by contracting. Muscle weakness, or fatigue, is the muscle's inability to produce as much force as it should. It may have its roots in a simple calcium leak from the muscle cell. *Wouldn't it be nice if it really were that simple?* However, a calcium "leak" is no simple matter. The scientists at Columbia University explain that this calcium then "eats away at the muscle fibers."

  Twenty percent of people experiencing muscle weakness and searching for answers through their doctor were found to be deficient in folate. If you find it difficult to make your body do specific tasks, like even lifting a small box off the floor, you may have a folic acid deficiency.

- **Irritability**—I get irritable anyway—that might come with homeschooling four of my children, not enough sleep, and no breaks from my schedule. It'd be kind of nice to have a good excuse… just not a medical one.

- **Loss of Appetite**—Your doctor doesn't have a specific test for "loss of appetite." There's no bloodwork, no urine test, and no scale you can stand on that will automatically tell him, "Yep. She can't eat, and this is why." Now, my children are pretty easy to figure out. If they're not eating there's something *seriously* wrong, and by the time that stage hits, we already know what it is. They usually eat non-stop. They're like Mac trucks! Your doctor, on the other hand, has to look at your records and kind of play the guessing game of which malady to test for next. Aren't you glad you can take your prenatals and rule out folic acid deficiency first?

Treating loss of appetite, until the supplement starts to do its job, begins with learning to plan out your meals. I sit down with my big desktop calendar and sales' ads every two Saturdays to plan out my meals for two weeks at a time. I then enter my meal list into Trello, where I also keep my meal list and shopping list, marking which things I have coupons for. This way I have it all handy on my phone (which I always have with me).

Your planned-out meals should be balanced, nutritious, and things you enjoy. This way, you'll eat them. We'll talk nutrition a bit later.

It'd be a great idea to fill your pantry with protein-rich, higher-calorie foods, getting them into your diet, and throw out the empty calories of the sugary items and junk food. If junk food isn't in your house, how will you eat it? If the healthy items are readily available, guess what you'll eat?

Homecooked meals make a difference too. In fact, you may be able to up your calorie count by 10% by just adding seasonings and sauces to your meal, and you can only do that if it's homemade. I tend to add garlic powder and seasoned salt or (less often) dried onion soup mix to most of my meals. I even add it to simple foods like macaroni and cheese. *The kiddos eat the fool out of that!* Cooking in real butter will also help.

Another thing I can suggest is getting your calories and nutrition by drinking your meals if you just *can't fit any more in your stomach.* Hey! I've been there! Protein drinks and green smoothies will do the job. Eating six to eight smaller meals all throughout the day instead of having three large meals will also be easier to tolerate.

Regardless of which ideas you follow, or don't follow, I hope you choose to eat a balanced diet. Getting all the food groups in and consuming the calories and nutrition you need will improve your appetite and your fatigue, which you are, no doubt, dealing with as well. Here's hoping the folic acid in your vitamins will kick in soon, and you'll be back to your usual self in no time.

- **Weight Loss**—Now, if you've lost your appetite and just can't bring yourself to eat, losing ten pounds would be nothing. However, if you've lost ten pounds OR if you've lost 5% or more of your healthy body weight over the course of six weeks or less, you may have a folic acid deficiency.

- **Heart Palpitations**—Have you ever had that feeling like your heart was going to pound out of your chest? Has it ever felt like it was racing to beat the band? Has it ever felt irregular, almost like it skipped beats? That can be a frightful experience, but it's usually harmless. Most "skipped heartbeats" are simply an early heartbeat followed by a short rest and a forceful heartbeat, which is where the flutter or "skip" comes from.

Unless it happens frequently, there's no reason to be concerned about it, it's just symptoms of a folic acid deficiency. If you are only deficient by a little, you may not even notice the heart palpitations, but, even at mildly deficient, you and your baby will still not be getting as much folic acid as you need. If you don't get these under control before you get pregnant, it may spiral out of control, not to mention, it can be detrimental to your baby!

BENEFITS

We talked about the bad things that go along with a folic acid deficiency—all the symptoms that go along with it. Now let's get a little more upbeat! Let's talk about the benefits of taking a folic acid supplement, one of the most important things you could do for yourself and for your baby-to-be!

To Your Baby

Do you want to prevent your baby from having spinal bifida or other serious spinal cord birth defects, which touch approximately 3,000 pregnancies across the states every year? NO?! Alright. I'll quit writing. JUST KIDDING! No, really. Taking folic acid will help prevent these disorders!

Not only that but if you take folic acid religiously and continue through your first trimester, you lower your baby's chance at getting neural tube defects (NTDs) by a whopping 70%! Who wouldn't protect their baby in this way if they could? Well, now you can!

Beginning to take a total of 400 mcg of folic acid daily before conception and 600 mcg after the pregnancy is confirmed to protect your child in many ways. Some say it'll lower his chances at getting cleft palate, cleft lip, or certain heart defects. It'll protect his developing brain and spine, beginning to do its job before you even have a clue you have a little life growing inside you.

Folic acid lengthens the amount of time that little bun stays in the oven, thus guarding against premature birth. This makes for healthier babies who also have more body weight to start out their lives.

Folic acid (folate) will help your baby on his journey toward development. It's a vitamin dubbed among the most important for development and growth. Due to this, it makes for a happy and healthy baby—one more likely to be free from the defects that come along with an unhealthy pregnancy driven by a folic acid deficiency. It will also aid in the growth of your baby-to-be's muscle tissue. Considered a factor in muscle building, it will benefit you as well!

Not only will regularly taking folic acid make sure your mind and your body are up and running, but it will *keep* it up and going too. It's kind of like a disk defragment, scan disk, and update on your computer. It unscrambles some of some past problems, smooths out the present issues, and prepares the future against some physical and emotional complications too. Let's look at a few!

Folate, or natural folic acid, is an antioxidant, attacking the free radicals in your body, one of the things that can cause cancer and other similar diseases. Cancer's ability to spread so quickly is thwarted by folic acid, helping your body in its fight against the start of cancer.

Folic acid is one of those vitamins that help to build and repair the skin cells and replace the old cells with new. *Did you know we get a whole new body every seven years because of cell repair, regeneration, and replenishment?* This nice little repair and replacement trick the folic acid pulls off keeps our body fresh and new. It also builds new red blood cells in the same way.

It increases the level of hemoglobin in your body, giving you more energy, which will come in handy when all those pregnancy hormones hit! It also raises your metabolism, helping you to burn those calories you intake when those cravings hit.

Just as this supplement readies your body to assist your baby in the development of his brain, it can also be used to treat your brain. It supports your body in stabilizing various emotional and mental disorders. Depression and anxiety are the two most prevalent mental disorders.

I'm sure you've heard about the baby blues. Well, believe it or not, we get depressed in pregnancy too. In fact, we can get depressed at any age and stage of life. I have Bipolar, so I've been depressed off and on since I was about sixteen. Less depression is seen among those who take folic acid regularly! To make a point here, doctors usually prescribe SSRIs, which are serotonin regulator drugs, to fight depression. Folate can stimulate the brain in the same way as moderate SSRIs do, battling depression on its own!

There are other ways folic acid will help you. Your body needs it to ward off a type of anemia that likes to rear its ugly head during pregnancy. It does this by making the red blood cells your body needs. It could also keep you from becoming one of that 5 % that get a severe blood pressure disorder pregnant women can get, called preeclampsia. It will aid in the cell growth needed to keep up with that rapidly growing placenta and soon-to-be rapidly developing baby inside your body! Last of all, folic acid is crucial for the getup and go and fix it up of our DNA—for the functioning, repair, and production. Our DNA is the genetic building blocks that make us "us."

Folic acid has some great benefits! Why wouldn't you want to use it? It'll help you, your future baby, and even your man. It'd be great for him to take it as well! I didn't cover everything it does for him, but check into it. Google it! It has incredible benefits for him, too.

CHAPTER THREE: SUPPLEMENTS—

YOUR PRENATAL AND IRON

My grandma always said her iron skillet was bowl-shaped because she used it to hit my grandfather on the head one too many times. My mom complained it was time to turn it over and hit him with the other side as the eggs slid to the edges of the pan, wiggling down into the cracks. She tried to pull them up into the center again for the third time as the unruly parts slipped away. Momma just threw her hands up in defeat and walked away. I took over.

"So why iron skillets anyway, Grandma," I asked. "I mean, they're so old. You never wash them—the whole seasoning thing… and they're so heavy. A new pan wouldn't be bowed, and they don't stick—at least the good ones. They're light, easy to wash, dishwasher-safe, and they don't rust, and **best of all** YOU CAN WASH THEM!!"

Grandma sighed, "I've always used cast iron. Iron's good for you."

You know what? It turns out she was right! Iron does happen to be good for you! Guess where you can find it? In your prenatal… and in your cast iron skillet!

IRON

No, I'm not talking about that thing we ladies supposedly use to press our business suits out. *Who does that anymore anyway?!* I'm not talking about the metal... you know, the one we most commonly know as steel these days—chemical element of atomic number 26 for all of you science buffs out there.

You know what I'm talking about. I'm just having a little fun. Iron is another one of those minerals your body needs and that you need even more during pregnancy... and, therefore, leading up to it! It's required to build connective tissue, like cartilage and collagen (an important building block in bone) and also for producing hormones. *I always wondered where **those** came from!* It helps you to stay well, helping to maintain that healthy immune system of yours or helping it get stronger to keep you and your baby-to-be healthier.

I. It's so important to have your iron levels right before you get pregnant because it's responsible for making you and your future baby develop and grow. You'll also need extra iron, in the last two-thirds of your pregnancy especially, for the growing of your baby and your baby's placenta.

II.   Iron produces two proteins: myoglobin and hemoglobin. Myoglobin carries oxygen to your muscles, while hemoglobin carries the oxygen your lungs produce into all the other parts of your body. You're going to need extra hemoglobin and 50% more blood than usual. Iron is responsible, to make this happen.

III. Iron is an essential part to the pieces of many other enzymes and proteins, supporting biological functions to the human body as well. These include energy production and DNA synthesis. They are in no way limited to this, as there are literally hundreds of others.

HOW MUCH IRON DO I NEED?

The amount of iron each person is supposed to get in their diet every day sorely depends on their age and stage of life. For instance, an infant, ages newborn to 6 months old, must have 0.27 mg of iron daily and the youth in our lives (ages 9-13) should be getting 8 mg a day. Now, as for those of you prepping your body, your daily goal should be for 18 mg per day. Once you get that positive pregnancy test, your goal will rise to 27 mg, and, if you choose to breastfeed, your requirements drop all the way down to 9 mg!

It's crucial for you to have your iron levels checked while you're prepping to see where you stand. Many of you will find your body is insufficient in this mineral and that you'll be starting out on the wrong foot, needing more iron to build up your stores.

There are those groups of people who, no matter how much iron-laden foods they eat, still have a difficult time consuming enough to satisfy their needs. For instance, if you are a Vegetarian who chooses not to eat seafood, meat, and/or poultry, you'll need almost twice the iron listed. Why? Our bodies cannot absorb the iron from vegetables as well as from that in meats. Other groups include:

- Those who donate blood frequently;

- Those with gastrointestinal (GI) disorders that cause poor nutrient absorption;

- Those with poor diets;

- Those with cancer;

- Those with heart failure;

- Those with heavy periods;

- And, of course, those who are pregnant.

These women should speak to their physician about taking an extra iron supplement.

SYMPTOMS

At first, there may be no real symptoms at all as your body gradually uses up what it has stored up. The scary thing is that these stores your body draws from are in the bone marrow, liver, spleen, and muscles. What do you think happens as those stores become low? Well, iron carries less oxygen to the lungs, muscles, and other parts of the body as iron deficiency anemia sets in. You see, without enough iron in your blood, it can't make enough hemoglobin.

While I was in my early third trimester with my second, Hannah, I began to feel faint all the time. I was tired non-stop. I knew something was wrong. Everyone told me that with a toddler running around and being in my second trimester it was normal to be tired. *Maybe, but not like this.* I brought it before my doctor.

"You're pregnant," he said, as a matter of fact, looking at me over his stylish black, rim glasses. "You're going to be tired."

The next visit, I brought it up again, but this time to my nurse. "How're ya doin' today," she asked. I could almost picture a piece of straw between her teeth and a straw hat on her head.

"Not so good." I've been exhausted." She took a breath to speak, but before she could, I held up my hands and started to talk again, "but not the normal exhausted. I'm really, truly, to the bone exhausted... and my head hurts. Annoyingly bad."

Sandy's mouth took on the straight line, and she narrowed her eyes and tilted her head as she always did when she was thinking. She stared at me for a second. "Let's get that iron checked for you today, Hun." She lightly patted my leg, turned, and left.

Sandy has always done me good. That time, she did Hannah *and* me a favor! The good Doctor Elliot took her suggestion and checked my Hemoglobin. It was low, as expected, and he started me on a prescription with orders to keep up with my prenatals as well. There are other symptoms of iron deficiency anemia other than tiredness. Let's explore them.

- **Tiredness and lack of energy**—I think we covered that pretty well.

- **Poor concentration and memory**—*I don't know. I think this pretty much comes along with pregnancy anyway. We always called it "Pregnancy Brain."*

- **Low immune system**—Since the hemoglobin in the red blood cells is necessary to distribute oxygen and other nutrients (including white blood cells—which is the immunity nutrient) to the rest of the body, you have an increased chance for infection and illness.

- **Less ability to control body temperature**—Oxygen failing to make it all the way to the hands and feet causes them to be cold all the time. Having cold hand and feet cause the rest of your body to be cold as well.

- **Sore Tongue**—In iron deficiency anemia, you don't have enough iron in your blood, so you're walking around red blood cell deficient. People who do not have iron deficiency anemia have enough of the hemoglobin (which is contained in the red blood cells you lack in). Hemoglobin is a protein that's rich in iron. It acts as a vehicle, transporting oxygen from the lungs to the tissues and back again. Those with iron deficiency anemia are at risk of ending up with tongue problems.

These problems include a tongue that's pale and smooth or a tongue that's sore, inflamed, and a swollen tongue. It can get challenging to swallow, chew, and even speak with a sore and swollen tongue.

- **Headaches**—If you get severe headaches or migraines from your iron deficiency anemia, you're not alone. With iron deficient anemia, there's a lack of sufficient hemoglobin due to the lack of enough red blood cells, as these blood cells are replenished and reproduced by iron. Remember how the hemoglobin's job is to transport the oxygen from the lungs to the tissues of the body? Well, without it doing its job, your brain's not getting enough oxygen. This, of course, produces headaches.

If you do get headaches or migraines, there are a few things you can do to combat them. These things include supplements, dietary changes, blood transfusions, and iron therapy. The great news is that, when the iron reserves are restored, iron deficiency anemia headaches usually go away by themselves.

You may need to seek other treatment or pain medications to help you out a bit until the iron supplements kick in. Some doctors recommend placing a warm compress on the back of your neck. Others say to use a cold one. Relaxation training, meditation, and massage are sometimes *just what the doctor ordered*. Rest in a dark, quiet room is sometimes welcomed and advisable if you can get it—My poor husband tries so hard to keep the kiddos quiet when I need to lay down, but when there are four children, there *will* be noise!

Sometimes, cognitive behavioral therapy (CBT) is also an accepted treatment. CBT aids the therapists in assisting their patients in catching, understanding, and changing their thoughts and feelings before they can influence their actions. Typically used to help in psychological cases, such as phobias, depression, addictions, and anxiety, CBT has been showing great strides in helping those of us who suffer from migraines. There's strong evidence that it helps us learn to control our migraines and the anxiety surrounding them, thus decreasing how often we have the headaches!

I'm glad I didn't get any further symptoms, and I'm so happy neither my baby nor I were affected by long or extreme iron deficiency, which could affect her in utero or even post birth—if she made it that long! *Yes, it can get that extreme!*

Some pregnant woman's iron level drops so low that it affects the health of their unborn baby or even their newborn himself! Low levels of iron while in the uterus or as a newborn may affect your baby's development. If you don't get enough iron, your baby might be affected by a low birthweight (*Hannah certainly wasn't! She was 10 pounds!*), premature birth (*She was in there until after her due date!*) or be born with low levels of iron himself. Some baby's whose mothers have low iron levels during pregnancy never make it at all or not for very long. Don't worry! If you catch it early enough, and even if you don't, there's plenty of time and plenty of hope!

Beyond all this, some Indian researchers have discovered that if you don't get enough iron, you can inhibit fertility by up to 60%! They found iron insufficiencies can keep you from ovulating and can even, possibly, cause your eggs to be in poor health. Iron is essential, and it can be supplemented through your prenatal.

IRON AND DIET

When Samuel, then either upper two or lower three-years-old, refused to take his vitamin, his doctor said, "Don't worry about it. Just feed him a balanced diet, and it'll all work out."

A toddler? A balanced diet? It'd all work out? Who was he kidding?

So we went to plan B—Grandma. She made it look so easy. She let him help choose the food, let him feel like he was helping to cook the food (He was just throwing the odds and ends away, but that made him happy), and let him help put his plastic plate on the table. Guess what? He ate every single bite!

We visited Grandma's a few more nights to make sure it wasn't some sort of fluke. When it worked each night for three nights in a week, we decided to try it at home. It worked seven times out of ten, but you know what? That was better than what we were getting!!

He started to feel better. After a while, he had more energy. *God forbid!* His nose didn't run non-stop, and he was beginning to ask for some of the _healthy_ foods for snacks! He finally started to chew up his vitamins and swallow them… just like his big sisters, but he was getting most of his nutrients through his food. This included his iron.

Iron-Containing food sources are divided into two forms of iron. These forms are called Heme and Non-Heme. Heme iron is much easier for you to absorb than Non-Heme. We can find heme iron only in animal sources, while non-heme iron can be found in eggs, dairy products, iron-fortified food, supplements, and plants. Let's explore some of these.

Just to remind you, we can only find heme iron in one place—
meat. As a note, one serving of meat is three-ounces. If you're out
and about and have no way to weigh it (*I mean, who wants to carry
a food scale with them and measure their food before the chef
cooks it anyway? How embarrassing...*) just remember that three-
ounces of meat is approximately the same size as the deck of
playing cards. (JUST A NOTE: Meat is weight *before* it is
cooked.) Here's some help:

- 1 serving of roast turkey, breast meat: 1.1 mg of heme iron

- 1 serving of roast turkey, dark meat: 1.1 mg of heme iron

- 1 serving of pork, loin chop: 1.2 mg of heme iron

- 1 serving of light tuna, canned: 1.3 mg of heme iron

- 1 serving of roast turkey, breast meat: 1.4 mg of heme iron

- 1 serving of roast turkey, dark meat: 2.0 mg: of heme iron

- 1 serving of lean beef, tenderloins: 3.0 mg of heme iron

- 1 serving of lean beef, chuck: 3.2 mg of heme iron

I'm sure you've heard how great of a source liver is supposed to be for your health, having a high concentration of iron. However, it is also high in vitamin A, which should be limited during pregnancy and during the prepping time of your body! You should only eat two servings a month at the most.

Non-Heme Iron

On that search for iron laden foods, you'll find the best foods to eat will be those like the poultry, red meat, and fish listed above, but some of you limit meat in your diet. If you're vegetarian or vegan or otherwise have a limited diet, you can still get your iron! Vegetables, grains, and legumes have iron in them as well, though they're not absorbed as efficiently into the body. Let's discuss some of these now.

The serving sizes of each vegetable differ so we will list them by amount, rather than by "serving." However, each listed is one serving.

- ¼ cup of raisins: 0.75 mg of non-heme iron

- One slice of whole wheat or enriched white bread: 0.9 mg of non-heme iron

- 1 cup of prune juice: 3.0 mg of non-heme iron

- ½ cup of spinach, boiled: 3.2 mg of non-heme iron

- ½ cup firm tofu, raw: 3.4 mg of non-heme iron

- 1 TBSP of blackstrap molasses: 3.5 mg of non-heme iron

- 1 cup pinto beans or black beans, cooked: 3.6 mg of non-heme iron

- 1 ounce of pumpkin seeds, roasted: 4.2 mg of non-heme iron

- 1 cup of lima beans, cooked: 4.5 mg of non-heme iron

- 1 cup of chickpeas: 4.8 mg of non-heme iron

- 1 cup of kidney beans, cooked: 5.2 mg of non-heme iron

- 1 cup of lentils, cooked: 6.6 mg of non-heme iron

- 1 cup of soybeans (also known as edamame), boiled: 8.8 mg of non-heme iron

- 1 cup of fortified instant oatmeal: 10 mg of non-heme iron

These numbers might impress you at first, but keep in mind that non-heme iron isn't absorbed as well. As a matter of fact, your body only absorbs 2-20% of the iron in that food, while heme iron will allow your body to absorb anywhere between 7 and 35%. The amount your body will absorb depends on iron deficiency. You absorb more when you're deficient and absorbing less when you have sufficient stores. Many other factors play roles in the amount of heme and non-heme iron absorbed.

GETTING MORE OUT OF YOUR IRON

Children are *always* looking to get more of *whatever* from *wherever* they can. It doesn't matter what it is or where it comes from. It's like they get that "Gimme-gimme disease"! *Gimme this! Gimme that! Gimme! Gimme!*

Well, my Samuel, when he was three, had no filters—like most kiddos at that age… well at most ages. There was a lady, Grandma Candy, who always brought (*yep! You guessed it!*) candy to church for all the kids. Samuel got so used to it that, one day, he ran up to Grandma Candy and spouted out, "What did you bring me today?"

Iron, both heme and non-heme, are like this. They've got the "gimme-gimme"s! They're needy little boogers. They need other things to make them function to the best of their abilities. The first thing they need is each other. Heme and non-heme iron are both needed in conjunction for you to receive a balanced, iron-fed diet. Poultry, red meat, and seafood, all three, include non-heme *and* heme iron. In fact, the iron content in meat is made up of only 40-45% heme iron. The other 55-60% is made up of the non-heme iron. There are also other dietary considerations.

- Add strawberries, broccoli, or even a glass of orange juice (any kind of vitamin C) to every meal. Vitamin C assists your body in absorbing more iron. It makes it into a sponge. When you add vitamin C to your meal, your body can absorb up to six times more iron!

- They say to take your iron supplement on an empty stomach with orange juice two hours before a meal.

- Be careful of certain foods. The phytates in legumes and whole grains, oxalates in spinach and soy foods, polyphenols in tea and coffee, and calcium in dairy products, are natural iron inhibitors. These are substances that make your body less able to readily absorb iron.

When you've been diagnosed with iron deficiency anemia or low iron, you may be warned against eating iron-rich foods and iron-inhibiting foods together. Other doctors may tell you that as long as your diet includes foods that are high in vitamin C, and as long as you get plenty of iron, it's absolutely fine to do so. *Don't you wish they'd make up their minds?* Talk to your doctor or nutritionist to come up with something that'll work for you.

- Here's another of those quandaries: Some physicians recommend their patients to take an iron supplement *and* a calcium supplement. (?) *Yeah… That's what I thought too.* Some of them suggest that you use an antacid, like TUMS, that has calcium in it, to control acid reflux. In this case, ask your provider how to space your supplements out throughout the day.

- Filling your plate with only one serving of meat (3-ounces) and the rest with other iron-rich foods helps you to absorb up the non-heme iron that makes up the rest of your meal.

SIDE EFFECTS

Like with everything, taking iron, or prenatals with iron in them, comes with a price—possible side effects. Some of these you might as well accept as fact. You may get constipated. You plan on getting pregnant, right? Well, know that this is a standard, pregnant woman problem, so get used to the idea. If you do end up "plugged up," as we call it around here, try to down some prune juice. Not only is it good for your constipation, but it's a good source of iron too. Many people don't like prune juice. I don't. However... something my kiddos like to parrot from a kid's program they listen too is, "What's good for ya ought to be good to ya!"

Some people have the opposite problem—diarrhea. If you do end up with it, there are several steps to combat it.:

- Drink plenty of clear fluids.

- If your diarrhea is mild, milk, which *can* prolong some cases, may help offer more nutrients to the poor, lonely soul.

- With moderate or severe cases, you should add electrolytes. You can achieve this by drinking things like Gatorade.

- Eat yogurt that is probiotic-laden. Some yogurt has active bacteria in it (*That just doesn't sound like happiness...*) that can lessen the symptoms of diarrhea.

- The BRAT diet (*Unfortunately, they're not talking about the tube-shaped meat...*) can help lessen the symptoms of diarrhea. This diet consists of restricting your intake of other foods and eating only *B*ananas, *R*ice, *A*pplesauce, and *T*oast.

- If you start to have symptoms of dehydration, which include weakness, dizziness, and muscle cramps, *please* see your doctor.

In the case of nausea, take your prenatal or iron supplement with a small snack or take it right before you go to bed. You might also consider eating small meals instead of full meals surrounding the times you're slated to take your supplements along with avoiding fried and fatty foods or very sweet foods close to time to take them since both these can make you nauseous as well. Make sure you're drinking a lot of fluids between meals to combat the nausea. Laying on an incline—not lying flat—will help while you're nauseous. You might also think about implementing some herbal remedies to help with nausea once it hits. Some of these might include:

- Drinking peppermint tea or placing peppermint oil under your tongue.

- Sipping on red raspberry leaf herbal tea steeped for at least 15 minutes,

- Drinking beverages, such as real ginger ale, made from real ginger.

- Eating pickled ginger or take ginger capsules.

Stomach pain is a side effect you might also *get* to "enjoy." In my opinion, this would go along with constipation or diarrhea. Here are a few natural remedies:

- Drink peppermint, ginger, or chamomile tea steeped for 15 minutes.

- Eat yogurt for the probiotics.

- Drink prune juice.

- Mix ½ of a cup of rice into six cups of boiling water, letting it boil until it's tender. Strain the rice out. Add a teaspoon of honey to a cup of rice water, and drink it. You can heat your rice water and sip on two cups every day.

- You can chew on ½ to 1 teaspoon of fennel seeds after each meal or crush 1 teaspoon of fennel seeds and make a tea out of it. Let the crushed seeds steep for 10 minutes, and drink it after each meal.

- *MY FAVORITE!!* Sip on warm lemon water.

- Use a hot water bottle on your stomach for 5-10 minutes at a time.

- Lastly, every woman's favorite for any ache or pain, take a **hot bath** or shower.

If you have anemia already, some stomach problems may be prevented by speaking with your doctor about starting with a lower dose of iron and slowly building upon that until you reach the amount you need to succeed. There are time-released supplements that might work for you, too, but, because they don't work as well, your doctor might also suggest taking smaller doses throughout the day to equal the same dose you would be getting if taken all at once.

You might find that you have black or dark-colored stools or dark urine. Dark "poo-poo" is actually a good thing. If it doesn't happen, that is cause for alarm. Dark stools testify to the fact that your body is successfully soaking up the iron like it's supposed too.

You might be graced with nagging headaches.

- Rubbing a few drops of peppermint and lavender essential oils on your temples, forehead, and the back of your neck may benefit you.

- If you take anywhere between 200 mg and 600 mg of Magnesium every day, this can help. The best news? You can continue using Magnesium when you get pregnant!

Upping your fiber intake will help you get your magnesium. Other things you can add to your diet to up your Magnesium levels are seeds, beans, squash, whole grains, nuts, leafy greens, and vegetables like broccoli.

Another unpleasant side effect would be an unusual or nasty taste in your mouth. *Girl, go brush those teeth!* You could try eating citrus fruits, like oranges or grapefruits. These are saliva-stimulating, which will help.

The best way to treat this side effect might be to try out a different brand of prenatals. If you're one of those to be blessed without a diagnosis of anemia and the iron level in your prenatal is over 30 mg, try one with less iron in it. If you are on prescription iron pills, ask your physician to prescribe a different brand of the same supplement.

Lastly, you really need to talk to your doctor if your side effects are too bothersome or if you have other side effects that worry you.

IRON? HARMFUL? NO WAY!

Yes way! We all know too little iron is bad, but did you know you can get too much iron? You should get less than 45 milligrams daily, whether it be from your prenatal, an extra supplement, or a combination of the two. Exceeding that amount can lead to Iron Overload, or Hemochromatosis, which can cause liver damage, arthritis, and diabetes if left untreated. It may have a part in leading to an imbalance in the body that may contribute to infertility and may possibly cause miscarriage and preeclampsia if not gotten under control before you get pregnant.

Getting too much iron can also cause oxidative stress. *Yeah, I had no clue what that was either...* When there is an imbalance between how many antioxidants and how many harmful free radicals are in our bodies, this produces Oxidative stress. Antioxidants are part of our defense system against free radicals.

Free radicals are molecules that are made up of one or more unpaired electrons that contain oxygen. They are so harmful because, being highly reactive, they can steal electrons. Doing this, they stabilize themselves but destabilize the cell components of the victimized molecules. These molecules then steal someone else's electron, then it's a free-for-all. One free radical triggers a chain of reactions that can lead to several different diseases and disorders from heart disease, chronic kidney disease, Parkinson's and Alzheimer's, and even all the way up to cancer!

*****

Just like with any other medication or harmful substance, KEEP YOUR IRON OUT OF THE REACH OF CHILDREN!! Iron in hundreds or even thousands of milligrams can bring about coma, organ failure, convulsions, and, yes, even death. Since the manufacturers have begun using child-proof packaging and warning labels, the number of accidental iron poisoning have decreased, but they still happen because of people not being careful enough.

INTERACTIONS

Any supplements or medications can interfere with any other drug or supplement you take. This is why it's so important that you always tell your doctor and pharmacist *every* medication or supplement you take!

"Here are several examples:

- Iron supplements can reduce the amount of levodopa that the body absorbs, making it less effective. Levodopa, found in Sinemet® and Stalevo®, is used to treat Parkinson's disease and restless leg syndrome.

- Taking iron with levothyroxine can reduce this medication's effectiveness. Levothyroxine (Levothroid®, Levoxyl®, Synthroid®, Tirosint®, and Unithroid®) is used to treat hypothyroidism, goiter, and thyroid cancer.

- The proton pump inhibitors lansoprazole (Prevacid®) and omeprazole (Prilosec®) decrease stomach acid, so they might reduce the amount of nonheme iron that the body absorbs from food.

- Calcium might interfere with iron absorption. Taking calcium and iron supplements at different times of the day might prevent this problem.

Tell your doctor, pharmacist, and other healthcare providers about any dietary supplements and prescription or over-the-counter medicines you take. They can tell you if the dietary supplements might interact with your medicines or if the medicines might interfere with how your body absorbs, uses, or breaks down nutrients." [Iron — Consumer - Office Of Dietary Supplements - Iron. (n.d.). Retrieved from https://ods.od.nih.gov/factsheets/Iron-Consumer/]

Chapter Four: Supplements—Your

Prenatal and Calcium

"More milk, peees?" I loved to hear the way Samuel said "please" at three, and I loved that he loved milk. Actually, he liked anything dairy—yogurt, cheese, you name it. He still does. Calcium is his thing! I am so thankful because some parents have to force their calcium-rich foods on their kiddos. I don't.

What is Calcium?

I think of calcium kind of like Samuel's building blocks—another one of his obsessions. It's what builds the strong bones, the framework of our body. Crucial to the top block of his tower, the base must be sturdy. Critical to living a healthy life, we must be sure to maintain a certain amount of calcium in our bodies. That is the base of our health. Thankfully, like the blocks populating Samuel's bedroom floor, waiting to be stepped on so I can limp away, calcium is the most plentiful chemical element in our bodies.

Now, we don't have any guarantee that our tower isn't going to fall over, but it has a much better chance of standing strong if we try to maintain it by keeping those blocks straight. Our bones stand a much better chance against weakness and breaks if we support them with the calcium they require. Since our bodies can't make calcium on their own, it needs that which can be supplied. We can do this by consuming at least three servings of foods that are rich in calcium daily.

CALCIUM-RICH FOODS

According to some research, only 10% of woman get enough calcium every day. This is a scary situation because of the ramifications of hypocalcemia (low calcium levels in your body). There are some easy ways to remedy this.

First, when you shop your shopping list, read your labels (*yes, I know we already covered this in previous chapters*). When choosing foods, choose the calcium-rich foods listed below, but also choose foods that are listed as "excellent source of calcium" or "calcium-rich." The other things you want to look for (and this is where your label reading comes in) is foods that have at least 10% of the DV (daily value) of calcium in them. During the prepping stage (and even during pregnancy), you should be getting around 1,000 mg of calcium a day.

There are several Western European and North American health authorities that recommend you get your daily calcium requirements from several sources, as this mineral can found in numerous foods and drinks. Several registered dietitian nutritionists have recommended that your primary source of nutrients, vitamins, and minerals—calcium being one of them, be from food. Harvard Medical School lists the following high calcium foods and their calcium values by milligram:

Produce	Serving Size	Estimated Calcium*
Collard greens, frozen	8 oz	360 mg
Broccoli rabe	8 oz	200 mg
Kale, frozen	8 oz	180 mg
Soy Beans, green, boiled	8 oz	175 mg
Bok Choy, cooked,	8 oz	160 mg

boiled		
Figs, dried	2 figs	65 mg
Broccoli, fresh, cooked	8 oz	60 mg
Oranges	1 whole	55 mg
Seafood	**Serving Size**	**Estimated Calcium***
Sardines, canned with bones	3 oz	325 mg
Salmon, canned with bones	3 oz	180 mg
Shrimp, canned	3 oz	125 mg
Dairy	**Serving Size**	**Estimated Calcium***

Ricotta, part-skim	4 oz	335 mg
Yogurt, plain, low-fat	6 oz	310 mg
Milk, skim, low-fat, whole	8 oz	300 mg
Yogurt with fruit, low-fat	6 oz	260 mg
Mozzarella, part-skim	1 oz	210 mg
Cheddar	1 oz	205 mg
Yogurt, Greek	6 oz	200 mg
American Cheese	1 oz	195 mg
Feta Cheese	4 oz	140 mg

Cottage Cheese, 2%	4 oz	105 mg
Frozen yogurt, vanilla	8 oz	105 mg
Ice Cream, vanilla	8 oz	85 mg
Parmesan	1 tbsp	55 mg
Fortified Food	**Serving Size**	**Estimated Calcium***
Almond milk, rice milk or soy milk, fortified	8 oz	300 mg
Orange juice and other fruit juices, fortified	8 oz	300 mg
Tofu, prepared with calcium	4 oz	205 mg

Waffle, frozen, fortified	2 pieces	200 mg
Oatmeal, fortified	1 packet	140 mg
English muffin, fortified	1 muffin	100 mg
Cereal, fortified	8 oz	100-1,000 mg
Other	**Serving Size**	**Estimated Calcium***
Mac & cheese, frozen	1 package	325 mg
Pizza, cheese, frozen	1 serving	115 mg
Pudding, chocolate, prepared with 2% milk	4 oz	160 mg

Beans, baked, canned	4 oz	160 mg

Another way you can increase your calcium intake is by crushing eggshells into a powder and adding them into your drink or food. Do be careful, because there are some foods, primarily a few dark green vegetables, that contain oxalic acid at high levels. This will make it harder for your body to absorb the calcium you ingest. *All that hard work lost, right?!*

THE BENEFITS OF CALCIUM

Calcium does so much for you. It's like a good friend that just won't quit coming around when you don't think you need the help!

"Leave me alone!"

"NO!" it argues back. "You need me, whether you know it or not."

Why?

- **Bone Health**—If you were to do a search and rescue for your calcium, you'd find about 99% of it in your teeth and bones. Your bone density is highest at 20 to 25-years-old, up until which time the calcium you intake has the role of the development, growth, maintenance, and strengthening of your bones. Bone density begins to decline after 25-years-old, which is all part of getting older, ladies. *Welcome to life as we know it.* Getting enough calcium will help your bones stay strong, slowing the bone density loss.

- **Muscle Contraction**—We all know how important the heart is, right? (*Do you remember that anti-drug commercial—"This is your brain." They show an egg. Then they say, "This is your brain on drugs" and* *smash the egg in a hot skillet. They finish the commercial by asking, "Any questions?"*) Well, "This is your heart (**thump, thump**). This is the heart without calcium (**eeeeeeeeeeee**). Any questions?" Calcium is what allows your muscles, all of them, to contract and relax. When your brain shoots that electric pulse down your nerve to your muscle, telling it to contract, calcium is released. The calcium works together with the proteins already in your muscle, making it finish the contraction. Your muscle can relax only when the calcium is expelled.

- **Blood Clotting**—It's definitely not hard to forget: knife slip equals cut, cut equals blood, blood equals band-aid. Easy, right? But... what keeps us from bleeding to death? I mean, why does our blood clot? Why don't we just run dry? Three substances working together save our lives—vitamin K, a protein called fibrinogen, and (*drumroll, please*) calcium! Without enough calcium, it would take quite a bit longer for your blood to clot. If you were lacking both vitamin K and calcium, it wouldn't clot at all.

- **High Blood Pressure**—Some research has been done showing that if you get the proper amount of calcium, it decreases your chances of getting high blood pressure. There was another large study done that proved people with high blood pressure can lower it by simply eating a specific diet, which just so happens to be calcium-rich—a diet high in vegetables, low-fat and fat-free dairy, and fruits.

- **Preeclampsia**—Causing high blood pressure and kidney problems, preeclampsia is a well-known, serious medical condition and one of those fears of pregnant women. Why? It's among the leading causes of sickness and even death in newborns and their mothers. Five to eight percent of American women will experience preeclampsia this year. Just this year alone, in America, about 76,000 pregnant women will die from it, 15% of babies will be born prematurely because of it, and 10,500 babies will die from it.

"THAT'S SCARY! HOW DO I KEEP FROM BECOMING ONE OF THE 5-8%?" Getting enough calcium reduces your risks of preeclampsia by a lot. The conclusion of thirteen separate studies concluded that pregnant woman could drastically reduce their risks of preeclampsia by taking 1,000 mg (or 1 g/d) of calcium daily if they're not getting enough in their diet. They also proved that taking this extra calcium, if necessary, made premature births less likely. However, most Americans have no problem whatsoever getting enough calcium.

SYMPTOMS OF DEFICIENCY

The milligrams of calcium you take isn't the only thing that matters. Many things affect how much your body actually absorbs. You could take 1,000 mg and be deficient, while your neighbor's daily diet, getting her 1,000 mg, may completely fill her needs. Some of the many factors that play into the amount your digestive tract actually absorbs are:

- **The amount of vitamin D you get**—the more, the better.

- **Your age**—you absorb less the older you get.

- **The ingredients in your food**—phytic acid, found in whole grains, and oxalic acid, found in some beans and veggies, actually minimize your calcium intake.

Negating your calcium intake with other ingredients, like phytic or oxalic acid isn't a big deal as long as you switch up your diet as stated above. If you don't though, it's important to watch out for those symptoms of calcium deficiency.

Deficiency symptoms aren't evident at first. You see, your body keeps your calcium levels regulated for a bit by stealing the calcium from your bones and teeth. This, of course, can lead to weak bones, resulting in fractures, and osteoporosis. If you don't get the right amount of calcium for too long, you may experience the following symptoms:

- Convulsions

- Finger Numbness

- Tingling in Your Fingers

- Abnormal heart rhythms

- Death

CALCIUM SUPPLEMENTS

God specifically put sufficient calcium in many foods to allow you to get enough to enable communication between your brain and your body. If you can't get enough calcium through your diet, there are products you can supplement with. If you're already deficient, I'm sure your doctor probably already recommended that you supplement with tablets to fill in that gap and to bring your stores up to sufficient levels. You don't want to go into pregnancy with insufficient calcium levels!

The vitamin and mineral industry is thriving. In fact, the National Institutes of Health did a study, finding that, among the 125.9 million adult women in the US (according to the last census—

2014), approximately 70% of us take dietary supplements. This includes calcium, which we women use to raise our daily intake by about 300 mg.

Ideally, you should get most of your calcium through foods, consuming no more than 600 mg in calcium supplements daily. You should separate your doses over two or three intervals throughout the day. You absorb the calcium better this way. You should also have something on your stomach when you take it, as that will aid in absorption as well. Another good thing about taking your calcium supplement with food is that it may help to minimize any side effects that may decide to toddle into your life.

*SIDE EFFECTS?! **GULP!***

There are five horrible symptoms if you fail to get enough calcium, but only three annoying side effects that you *might* experience if you take something to prevent yourself from becoming horribly deficient. These are:

- Bloating;

- Constipation;

- Gas;

- Or, any combination of the three.

I'd rather face the possibility of side effects than the symptoms of a deficiency!

It's best to choose a supplement that uses calcium citrate rather than calcium carbonate since the former has fewer side effects and because they are less pronounced. As mentioned earlier, taking fewer milligrams at a sitting and taking it with food will help.

WHICH SUPPLEMENT?

There are so many supplements out there with calcium in them! Which one is best? There are multivitamin-minerals, calcium, and calcium with vitamin D. Then there are calcium carbonate and calcium citrate. Other supplements have calcium in the form of lactate, gluconate, and phosphate. Which supplement is best? It can be frustrating trying to figure it out!

The first thing that sheds light on the validity of a supplement for me is their seal of verification—those things like "USP Verified" and "NSF Certified." *Why are there so many seals of approval anyway?!* Sharon Akabas, Ph.D., the associate director initiatives at Columbia's Institute of Human Nutrition, said that "no supplement seal guarantees the safety or effectiveness of the ingredients in the bottle," though the manufacturers attempt to reassure you through words like "certified," "verified," and "approved."

The organizations that certify the supplements, like U.S. Pharmacopeia and NSF International, aren't guaranteeing the therapeutic value of them. *Well, what good are they then?* They *do* certify, however, that the bottle has in it what it says it does and that the supplements don't carry any contamination with them. These contaminates that other supplements are not promised to be free of would include arsenic, bacteria, or lead. The four seals you might see are consumerlab.com, NSF International, U.S. Pharmacopeia, and UL.

The next thing to do is to check the label. Does it contain vitamin D? Vitamin D will help your body better process the calcium you take in. How many milligrams of calcium does it have in it? Somewhere around 300 mg is best.

Check the active ingredients. Does it contain calcium carbonate or calcium citrate? If you have low levels of stomach acid, you want calcium citrate. Calcium carbonate is cheaper. If you use it (I'm sure you will be in the form of Rolaids ® or Tums ®, during pregnancy... *trust me*), make sure to have something on your stomach if you want it to be adequately absorbed. Though calcium citrate is more expensive, it'll be absorbed well, regardless of whether your stomach has food on it or not.

In other words, there's no one supplement that's necessarily "the best." The best one for you is the one that works best for your needs. What kind of certification do you want? How many milligrams do you need? What type of calcium will work best for you? Do you want to have to eat something with it? Do you need cheap? Are you having side effects? Which brand is easiest on your stomach? Do you need a multivitamin or a stand-alone mineral—maybe, if you need to spread your calcium up into two doses, you could think about doing a multivitamin with 300 mg of calcium in the morning with breakfast and a calcium with vitamin D supplement of 200 or 300 mg with supper. The real question is, which is best for *you*?

CALCIUM-BOOSTING TIPS

Many foods have calcium in them. Here are some ways to incorporate those calcium-laden foods into your daily diet.

- Prepare your oatmeal with milk.

- Top your baked potato with a ¼ of a cup of shredded cheese.

- Make a snack of dried figs or cooked soybeans.

- If you're going to eat tofu, make sure it's calcium-fortified.

- Find ways to add calcium-rich greens to your meals— you'll find a list of those above.

- Blend a calcium-fortified drink, or you can use milk, with greens or fruits to make a breakfast shake.

- Make a breakfast or snack of yogurt.

- Instead of having soda pop or sweet tea with your meals, have milk, orange juice, or another calcium-fortified drink.

- **Just as a reminder:** to boost your body's absorption and calcium retention power, get more vitamin D in your diet and/or through supplements.

CAN I GET TOO MUCH CALCIUM?

The simple answer? Yes. We have established that getting too little calcium is bad for you. *Remember "Thump-thump… Eeeeeeee…"* Getting too much calcium isn't good either. Although not yet well-established, it's known that getting too much could affect your body's ability to absorb other vitamins and minerals, particularly zinc and iron. This would cause you to be deficient in those areas—not good either… *Have you ever heard that saying, "Robbing Peter to pay Paul?"*

Getting too much could constipate you. It causes poor bone health and poor heart function, in fact, it may be linked to heart disease. It may cause your brain to function poorly. There is also research pointing to possibilities that it may possibly be a cause in prostate cancer. Getting too much calcium may also up your chance at kidney stones; getting "too much" from food doesn't do this.

You should be getting around 1,000 mg of calcium per day but can safely intake 2,500 mg daily without complications. It's tough to get too much from diet alone. When people overdose on calcium, it's through calcium supplements.

SYMPTOMS OF HYPERCALCEMIA

We must be careful because Hypercalcemia (the medical name for high levels of calcium) carries with it the big consequences I listed above. One I didn't mention is that having a serum calcium concentration level above 14 mg/dL (3.25 mmol/L, as is used in Canada, Europe, and Asia) which is considered extremely high, can be life-threatening. A normal adult level is between 9.4 mg/dL (2.35 mmol/L) and 9.9 mg/dL (2.475 mmol/L).

Mild hypercalcemia, levels above 10 mg/dL (2.5 mmol/L), but less than 14 mg/dL (3.5 mmol/L), may not result in any symptoms at all. However, adults with serum calcium levels above 14 mg/dL may have the following side effects:

- It can give you stomach issues such as nausea, constipation, abdominal pain, and vomiting.

- It can leave its fingerprints all over your brain, causing lethargy, confusion, and fatigue.

- Hypercalcemia can also cause mental health issues, like depression and anxiety.

- High calcium levels can cause your kidneys to over-work while trying to rid your body of the extra calcium.

- You end up running to the bathroom to pee every few minutes due to the overworking of your kidneys. You'll feel like you're already pregnant—you don't want that excessive urination right *now*! Get this thing right so you can at least have some peace before having to waddle to the potty later!

- The overworking of your kidneys will cause dehydration, which, in turn, will cause excessive thirst. *And... there's more peeing. Does it ever stop, people?*

- Hypercalcemia can also change the rhythm of your heartbeat, adding strain to your heart.

- It can raise your blood pressure, which puts more strain upon your heart. *Like you need your blood pressure high **before** you start trying for a baby...*

- Lastly, high levels of calcium do the opposite of what you'd think. Instead of making the bones stronger, it actually caused your bones to release calcium, causing muscle weakness and bone pain *and* making your bones weaker.

It's vital for you to get your calcium levels under control before you leave the prepping stage. Whether your levels are high or low, there can be complications, and neither you nor your baby need that. You owe it to yourself, your man, and your baby-to-be to go into this as healthy as you can be.

INTERACTIONS

Always, always, *always* talk to your doctor and pharmacist before starting any new supplement. *Have I hounded this enough yet?* Calcium supplements can interact with some medication, either causing the medicine to not work as well, activating an interaction, or prompting the calcium levels in your body to do weird things.

- Calcium levels do weird things when diuretics get involved. Diuretics are not created equal either. They don't play fair. They have different effects depending on what type they are:

- Loop diuretics (Bumex ® and Lasix ®, for example) will lower your serum calcium levels since they increase calcium excretion.

- Diuretics such as Lozol ® or Diuril ® (thiazide-type diuretics), however, will raise your serum calcium levels. They reduce calcium excretion.

- When used for months at a time, glucocorticoids, like prednisone, can deplete your calcium, bringing on osteoporosis!

- The absorption of some medications can be reduced if you take it at the same time as you take the following prescriptions:

  - Antibiotics belonging to the tetracycline or fluoroquinolone families;

  - Phenytoin, which is an anticonvulsant;

  - Bisphosphonates, which doctors use to treat osteoporosis;

  - Levothyroxine, which treats thyroid activity;

- o And, tiludronate disodium. The doctors use this to treat Paget's disease.

- Calcium absorption can be reduced by stimulant laxatives and mineral oil.

- You lose more calcium in your urine than usual when taking antacids that have magnesium or aluminum in them.

When I was pregnant with Hannah, my second, I had horrible heartburn (I had it with ALL of them. I have GERD, though, and that doesn't help). One day, I thought life was going to end. I had run out of TUMs. I looked everywhere in my house. Nothing. They were nowhere. I couldn't leave to go get some. I was car-less. My husband's was in the shop, and he had mine at work. Now that I think about it, though, I'm not sure if it would've been wise to go out alone—several months pregnant and having a toddler. You see, we had just had a horrible snow storm the day before, and the snow was deep and heavy.

I had called him at work to purchase me some, but I had to wait until he got home for my heartburn relief. The wait had been torturous, and I'd tried everything I could think of to ward it off, but nothing had worked. Now that I know what happens to me, I'm glad I didn't get those TUMs when I thought I needed them. I ate them like candy as it was.

When my husband showed up, he brought none other than fruit-flavored TUMs. Now, you have to understand I hate those things. They taste like sweet chalk to me. I have to have the mint kind. The mint kind is yummy. The mint kind I can stomach. The variety-flavored... not so much. He made me eat every last one of those before he'd buy me another mint-flavored bottle, and he'd purchased the largest size the pharmacy had, not knowing I disliked them! You see, finances were very tight, and he knew if he didn't do that, they wouldn't get eaten, so I had agreed. It had slowed down my habit of popping those TUMs though! Once I got my mint flavored TUMs back, I was right back at it.

I started to have dizzy spells. I almost passed out a few times, landing on my bottom on the floor, half blacking out on the way down and having to crawl to the freezer and stick my head inside to cool myself down to keep myself from vomiting. I've had problems with keeping my blood sugar levels up since I was a teen, so I assumed it was my hypoglycemia. I mean, why not, right?

I started having trouble with my equilibrium. I started bouncing off the walls when I walked. My mom was convinced I had vertigo. I didn't question her wisdom. She had vertigo, so why not?

I started to get constipated and to have horrible stomach cramps. They were awful. I sought help from the older ladies in my church. "Oh, it comes with pregnancy," they said. I reached out to my friends on Facebook, asking what you can do for stomach cramps. A friend from college suggested sipping hot water with lemon in it. It worked like a charm. I didn't question it.

I started to hurt all over. Again—"It comes with late pregnancy," the older women said.

"You have Ehler's Danlos," Momma said. "That makes your daddy hurt too."

"It's because of the cold temperatures," said the internet. We lived in Michigan. It was twenty below outside with windchill. My wall furnace, too small for the house, had a hard time keeping up. Consequently, it was 65 degrees in my house. *Why not?* I didn't question it. I was miserable.

I went into preterm labor. I went to the hospital, and they stopped it with medication. The doctor asked about my symptoms. He asked why I hadn't told him before. I explained what everyone had said. He said, "Hmph." He didn't question it, and I went home.

I went into preterm labor again. Again, I went to the hospital. Again, they stopped it. Again, they asked me about my symptoms. I repeated myself. My doctor didn't question it. I was put on bedrest.

When I went into preterm labor the third time, I was around 32 weeks along. I ended up with a different doctor at that time. He ran a different test. He tested my blood calcium levels. They were too high. He found the problem. I'd been taking prenatals, taking a calcium supplement with vitamin D, sticking close to my oranges, eating the fool out of Oreos with, of course, milk, and popping my TUMs.

I stopped the calcium supplement, limited my intake of TUMs, which I didn't need as much since the doctor banned me from eating so many oranges, and was forced to cut down on my steady diet of Oreos, which meant less milk… My calcium levels came down, and Hannah made it to her due date. In fact, when she got there, she didn't want to come out! We had to induce her… late. We were blessed. Be careful, ladies, of that consumption—not too little, not too much.

CHAPTER FIVE: SUPPLEMENTS—YOUR PRENATAL AND VITAMIN C

Momma used to push our fruits and vegetables on us all the time. "You need your vitamins," she'd say. Of course, Momma always got her way. We ate them. She juiced them. We drank them and had the pulp in pies and salads. We had them with each meal. It seemed we were never sick. Could it have had anything to do with the vitamin C in them, or was it just plain, old luck?

You hear about vitamin C all the time—taking vitamin C when you have a cold, using vitamin C to boost your immunity, eating oranges for vitamin C, and more, but why exactly do you need it? Does it really work? How will it help during your future pregnancy? Will it help your baby-to-be?

VITAMIN C

Your body can't make vitamin C (also known as L-ascorbic acid), so it must be ingested. It's readily available to you through two avenues: foods and supplements. It's naturally present in some foods and added in others as to offer you more of an opportunity to get your daily quota. *I guess they don't think we can do it on our own...?*

WHY DO I NEED IT?

I've talked to you a lot about how important the many different vitamins are, but I'm sure you've heard so much about Vitamin C just going about your daily life that you probably don't even need me to expound on that. Everyone has their opinions on vitamin C—good things and scary things. Let's explore some of these things.

First, why does your body even need vitamin C?

- The most known benefit is that it boosts your immune system, helping your body to fight viruses and infection. According to some research, vitamin C might help cut how long your cold will stick around. My father-in-law swears by it. Scientists say that in order to get this benefit, you must have already been taking the vitamin before the cold hit.

- If you're going to heal from those cuts and scrapes, whether nasty or minor, you must have vitamin C in your body. In fact, you can't have healthy skin at all without it.

- It's essential for bone healing, so unless you plan to keep that fractured bone forever, make sure to get enough vitamin C. It's vital for strong bones (and teeth) at all. It also builds those strong bones for your future baby-to-be.

- It assists your body in absorbing more iron, which you've already learned is also very important to your diet.

- It'll help your baby-to-be in his growth process. You see, it's a vital part of the collagen making process. Collagen is a necessary ingredient in the building of tendons, cartilage, skin, and, of course, bones.

You need to be consuming plenty of vitamin C every day, whether through foods or vitamins… or both. This is important to your health and development and, as you will see later, the development of your future baby-to-be.

AMOUNTS

The low limit for you would be 75 mg, and the high limit would be 2,000 mg. Upon pregnancy, you will need at least 85 mg. After giving birth, if you decide to breastfeed, you will only need 120 mg a day. If you're a smoker, you must raise that daily need by 35 mg more. These values are so simple to meet! For instance, just 8 ounces of orange juice contains 124 mg of vitamin C!

SOURCES

The best place to get your vitamin C is through food. There is a lot of it in citrus fruits. Many other fruits, leafy greens, and vegetables are great places to round it up too. You can also find some juices and cereals that are fortified with vitamin C. You should eat your fruits and vegetables fresh since cooking them will destroy the vitamin C. You should try to eat a food that contains a good amount of it with each meal. There are several good vitamin C sources listed below:

Type of Food	Serving Size	Amount of Vitamin C
Orange juice	8 oz.	124 mg
Bell pepper, chopped, raw, sweet red	one-half cup	95 mg
Papaya	one fruit	93.9 mg
Strawberries	one cup	84.5 mg
Orange	one medium fruit	70 mg
Grapefruit juice	three-quarters cup	70 mg
Kiwifruit	one medium fruit	64 mg
Green pepper, sweet, raw	one-half cup	60 mg

Broccoli, boiled	*one-half cup*	*58.2 mg*
Brussels sprouts, cooked	*one-half cup*	*48 mg*
Broccoli, raw	*one-half cup*	*39 mg*
Grapefruit	*one-half medium fruit*	*38 mg*
Tomato juice	*three-quarters cup*	*33 mg*
Raspberries	*one cup*	*30.7 mg*
Cantaloupe	*one-half cup*	*29 mg*
Mango	*one-half fruit*	*28.7 mg*
Boiled cabbage	*one-half cup*	*18.2 mg*
Boiled beet greens	*one-half cup*	*17.9 mg*

Potato, baked	*one medium*	*17 mg*
Tomato	*one medium*	*16 mg*
Spinach, cooked	*one-half cup*	*9 mg*
Spinach, raw	*one cup*	*8 mg*
Green peas, frozen, cooked	*one-half cup*	*8 mg*

SUPPLEMENTS

Another source of vitamin C is supplements, but should you really take them? If you're already taking prenatal vitamins, which you should be, then definitely not. If you're getting a diet high in vitamin C but not taking prenatals, then probably not. Your prenatals have enough in them to fulfill your quota if you also eat according to the nutritional guidelines (We'll get into that in the next chapter).

The safest way to get your vitamin C during pregnancy is through food. Remember that you can get above your low-end quota by drinking a glass of orange juice every morning with breakfast. Although some research has proved that using vitamin C can cut the frequency of premature rupture of membranes (PROM), there are also some worries that these supplements may **not** be good for pregnancy. The reasoning behind this is because having too much vitamin C could cause preterm birth. "Too much?" How much is "too much?"

VITAMIN C OVERDOSE

Yes, you can overdose on vitamin C. Seems pretty crazy, right? I mean, you need it... How can you OD? The answer is, "The same way you can on any other medication, vitamin, or mineral."

You can have up to 2,000 mg of vitamin C a day. *My soul, that's a lot of oranges!* Anything above that is overdosing. Mega-doses of it can give you:

- Nausea;

- Heartburn (*Duh! It's acid!*);

- Insomnia;

- Diarrhea;

- Vomiting;

- A headache;

- And, abdominal cramps.

VITAMIN C DEFICIENCY

On the other end of the spectrum, if you don't get enough vitamin C, you could be in trouble and so could your future baby-to-be. The symptoms of a vitamin C deficiency include many yucky symptoms:

- Your gums may be inflamed.

- You may find yourself fatigued

- Your cuts may heal more slowly.

- You may bruise more easily.

- Your skin may be rough and dry.

- Your joints may begin to ache.

That sounds like me! Maybe I should get checked? ...or perhaps I'm just getting old...

If you get less than 10 mg of vitamin C daily, you will develop scurvy. Scurvy is very rare in developed countries. However, it does still happen in people with poor food variety. In the mid-1700s, a British Navy Surgeon by the name of Sir James Lind learned that eating or drinking citrus could take care of scurvy. In 1932. Scientists finally discovered the active component in the citrus fruits that cured the scurvy was ascorbic acid—or, vitamin C.

If you're not getting enough vitamin C in your diet, you'll need to adjust your diet so you are before you reach that "bun in the oven" stage. It's essential. Being deficient during pregnancy can carry with it some pretty hefty consequences:

- Damage of Capillary veins

- Scurvy

- Complications in your baby-to-be's brain

- Possible impaired mental development in your newborn

There are several groups of people at risk of becoming deficient, including those who have limited food variety. For instance, the elderly may not have the ability to purchase as many fruits and vegetables as they need to in order to meet their dietary requirements because of their limited income. People who abuse alcohol or drugs may not get the nutrients necessary since those substances steal the vitamins from their body and keep their body from absorbing vitamins that they **are** consuming. Food faddists may avoid specific foods that are needed to obtain their vitamin C.

Those with chronic diseases, such as malabsorption, may need more vitamin C than others. This may make it harder for them to reach their daily values. This also includes people with cachexia, some cancers, and those with end-stage renal disease on chronic hemodialysis.

WARNING!

Side Effects

We've already spoken about the possible side effects of prenatal vitamins. Just like any other vitamin, mineral, or medication, taking an extra vitamin C supplement can result in one or more side effects. Here are a few of the common ones:

- You could get a headache.

- An upset stomach while eating or after you finish is possible.

- Your skin may get red and have a warm feeling, otherwise known as flushing.

- You could get nausea, vomiting, and/or diarrhea.

- A faint feeling is possible.

Scary Effects!

Besides this, there are two cases in which you must be very careful about taking a vitamin C supplement or even keep from taking a supplement at all.

- Do not take a vitamin C supplement if you're allergic to any ingredients in it—especially ascorbic acid, which is the active ingredient. *Do I really even need to state this one?*

- If you have kidney problems, taking high doses of vitamin C increases your chance of developing a rare condition called hyperoxaluria. Hyperoxaluria is serious. It causes too much oxalic acid to be expelled through urination. This also raises your chances of getting kidney stones.

I got a kidney stone when I was pregnant with Samuel, my fourth and last. I thought I was in early labor. After having two miscarriages and then going into premature labor so many times with Hannah, my second, that is not something we wanted to play around with. We rushed to the hospital. We were so relieved with the kidney stone diagnosis, but I was still in pain for a few days. Kidney stones are not anything you want to deal with! Besides, as I said earlier, if you're eating a balanced diet and taking your prenatal, you don't need an extra vitamin C supplement anyway.

You must remember that every vitamin has the possibility of interacting with other vitamins or medications. Make sure you tell your doctor and pharmacist. This goes with anything... even vitamin C. I take a few psychological drugs, and I can't even take cough medicines or over the counter acid reflux medications! I'm so glad I asked my pharmacist before I did!

Some medications definitely kick you out of the running for taking an extra vitamin C. The IV infusions of deferoxamine (Deferal) is one of these. Then, there are those medications that you shouldn't take a vitamin C tablet, over and above what you're getting in your prenatal, with due to interactions. These include:

- Ferrous gluconate (Ferralet, Fergon, Ferate)

- Warfarin (Coumadin)

- Exjade (deferasirox)

- Birth control pills containing some forms of ethinyl estradiol, estradiol, or mestranol

- Ferrous sulfate (Fer-Gen-Sol, FeoSol, and Fer Iron)

To recap: vitamin C is good. You need vitamin C. Your future baby-to-be needs vitamin C. You get enough vitamin C through your diet and prenatal vitamin and do not need a stand-alone supplement. You must be sure to get enough vitamin C, but that is simple to do. You need to get at least 75 mg every day. Getting too much vitamin C is bad, but you have to get 2,000 mg of vitamin C to reach that mark, and that's hard to do without trying. In fact, that would take eating 28 ½ oranges a day!

Be sure your vitamin C levels are right by being sure you eat a healthy, balanced diet and taking your prenatal vitamin on a regular basis. "Healthy diet?" you might say. "Balanced diet?" Being a mommy of four, I've become a circus act. Six years ago, however, I couldn't balance three plates in one hand and serve with the other, never mind balance a diet, so... "How do I eat a balanced diet to get the right amount of vitamin C anyway?" *Yay! I'm so glad you asked! Next chapter, please!*

CHAPTER SIX: FOR HEALTH'S SAKE

People used to get all the nutrients they needed from food, but nowadays, they eat junk food, junk food, and more junk food. Sure, America tries to make up for it by fortifying our grains and drinks with differing vitamins, but nothing makes up for the real thing. We need the real, honest to goodness sources of vitamins that come from real food to accompany our prenatal supplement if we are going to prep our body correctly.

When my friend, Kim's granddaughter came to visit her once, Kim gave her chocolate milk in her sippy cup thinking she'd be overjoyed! After all! It was **chocolate milk**! Every kid likes chocolate milk, right? Kim handed her the sippy with a smile on her face. Her granddaughter eagerly reached out to grab the sippy, took one look at it, and threw it on the floor. Confused, Kim picked the cup back up and offered it again. Her granddaughter knocked it out of her hand onto the floor and said, "Dirty milk!" in an angry tone. She was so mad at Kim for giving her "dirty milk"! Come to find out, she had never had chocolate milk before, as her mom wasn't big on sugar. She was not happy until she had real milk. Our bodies are not truly happy until we have the real food. Get in the habit of feeding it the real thing now while you're still in the prepping stage!

NUTRITION

Are you one of those people who skip meals, thinking it'll make you thinner? You're sabotaging yourself! It actually slows down weight loss and makes your body unhealthy. Are you one that just gets so busy that night is upon you before you realize lunch has even passed you by? You must make time to eat! How are you going to keep up with your busy lifestyle or have a healthy pregnancy if your body is unhealthy and unbalanced?

HAVE A PLAN

So, confession time. What have you been eating? Hopefully not everything but the kitchen sink. Are you a junkaholic—stuck on potato chips, cheesy puffs, twinkies, candy bars, and Oreos? Are you a tv dinner kind of person? Do you cook out of boxes—convenience meals to the rescue? What about fast food? Do you stick to all vegetables, avoiding all else in an attempt to lose weight? The real question, here, is, what **should** you be eating? Good question!

I used to have some form of nutritional plan. I mean I grew up on a 300-acre horse and cattle ranch until I was nine-years-old. We were well supplied with eggs, fresh produce, and fresh meat and with milk from down the street at the dairy farm. We traded eggs for those.

During the next few years, after a move, my parents implemented the Halleluiah diet. It's a health-based diet that has a lot to do with juicing to get all your vegetables for the day among other things. Fast forward a little, and my family lived on a farm in West Virginia for a few years, where we had laying hens and milk goats. We had a garden there too. It was there that we had taken up the vegetarian diet, also continuing to stick pretty close to the Halleluiah diet as well. We juiced all sorts of vegetables, did barley greens, ate crushed egg shells (...*I know...Weird, right?*), drank sassafras tea from roots we dug up, harvested our own herbs and spices, picked our own mushrooms and ramps, and more. Don't worry, we got our protein through our eggs, beans, sunflower seeds, and nuts.

Having grown up with such health-conscious parents, you'd think I would be a pro at this nutritional eating thing, right? Wrong! When I left home for college, the college food, which was all I could afford (that and Roman Noodles) was lacking in nutritional value.

After four years of that, I married. We both worked. Between that, the extracurricular activities I was expected to participate in for my students (I taught in a Christian school, and they required quite a bit), my husband's college schedule, grading papers, caring for my classroom after school hours, and my martial arts classes, we were busy critters. We were never home, so we ate fast food for almost every meal—*not healthy!*

Upon graduation, my husband I began working in the ministry helping small and struggling churches, which, and I'm not complaining, doesn't pay well. Our food budget was very limited, so our fruit and vegetable intake consisted of what WIC, the state program, supplied for breastfeeding women. It wasn't much.

It wasn't until about four years ago that I became health conscious once more. I started exercising again, eating healthy, and training my children what I had learned when I was young. We actually have the money to get the fresh fruits and vegetables we need. We are well on our way back to health.

I know you hear it a lot, but shop the outside of the store. Stay out of the middle aisles. Eat fresh. Stay away from processed foods as much as you can. Cooking homemade is so much healthier for you than eating boxed dinners, like "Hamburger Helper" or tv dinners. Just the salt in them alone will become an enemy to your kidneys and a hunting assassin to your blood pressure. The chemicals in processed foods and the fact that they don't have those natural vitamins and minerals in them that your body needs will not help you in your venture toward building your body toward a healthy vessel for carrying your beautiful baby either.

I know you're not eating for two yet, but it's important that your refrigerator is stocked up with healthy foods, foods that are chock-full of the nutrients you and your future baby will need throughout your pregnancy. You must shoot for a total of at least 2 ½ cups of vegetables and two cups of fruit every day. Protein is essential to your health as well, so you must be careful to get protein from a variety of sources. Some of these sources might include nuts, soy products, beans, seeds, meats, and poultry. You should also be sure to get foods like calcium-fortified orange juice, milk, yogurt, and other high calcium foods. You need to get an adequate amount of whole grains as well.

If you don't see any foods on the list that you like, don't worry! You'll find something. Everything isn't listed. There are so many choices! Everything you're used to can be made homemade with natural ingredients and made so much healthier, though I wouldn't suggest some of the things. Although you can make your own French fries, potato chips, and deep-fried chicken, it's much better, health-wise, to stay away from those, or at least not to eat them very often. If there's something you disliked before, try it again. You might enjoy it the second time around, and you may discover a new food you never knew you liked before today!

My children hate eating certain foods—especially Samuel (5-years-old). He's so picky! He still eats those things since I never make anything extra or different for anyone just because they don't like something. Not long ago, he just up and decided he doesn't like spaghetti anymore. My 10-year-old made spaghetti yesterday with egg noodles—*Yes, I'm teaching my girls to cook.* He ate his required half of scoop and took his plate off the table.

"Don't you want more?" my husband asked.

"No," he replied, "I don't like spaghetti."

I told him it wasn't spaghetti. It was made with different noodles.

He brought his plate back to the table and tried it again. He ended up eating more of that than I did!

Exercising

A good habit to get into at any stage of life, exercise will help you reach your healthy weight while awaiting the "stuffing the sheets" stage, that time where you're trying to conceive that baby-to-be. Being a healthy weight is beneficial to a healthy pregnancy and will actually make it easier to conceive.

If you're a healthy weight when you start your pregnancy, you'll be getting it off on the right foot. Women who are overweight have higher chances at problems popping up during pregnancy, and those still overweight at the end are more subject to having complications during delivery. And... being underweight may cause your future baby to be born underweight, but you have time to correct that now—or at least to start.

The director of the infertility service at the Cleveland Clinic, James Goldfarb, MD, said that you can increase your chances of pregnancy through moderate exercise. If you're going to be at a point where you can do moderate exercise daily by the time you're ready to start trying for that beautiful baby, you must start out small now and begin working up to your goal. An example of moderate exercise might be speed walking at least five days a week for thirty minutes a day.

To keep up with your daily exercise, you'll need an exercise program to follow. Create one that will satisfy your needs. Talking to a personal trainer might be beneficial in the creation of this plan. Another option is Google. Many sites on there offer ideas on how to build your own exercise program. Some of them have exercise programs already laid out for you. There are videos on YouTube or on purchasable videos that you can follow along with as part of your program. I like my Tae Bo cardio DVD.

When building your exercise program, there are some things you'll want to consider:

- **You must create a plan that's doable.** This means writing a schedule that'll work for you. You'll want to exercise for five days and rest for two. Next, you'll want to take two days that are lighter days (These will include less strenuous exercises, like casual swimming or Yoga). I use Sundays and Wednesdays as "off" days, or rest days, because of the restriction of time due to church.

- **You should switch it up.** Having the same exercise every day will get boring, and, soon, a lack of motivation will begin to set in. Also, exercising your whole body is essential. Switching up which exercises you do will switch up which muscles you work. I like to cycle between cardio, using my Tae Bo DVD, strength training, and HIIT (high-intensity interval training). You might try using Leslie Sansone's YouTube videos (*I love me some free!*) for walking if you can't get out and only have a small place to exercise in. You might also consider speed walking, biking, and rollerblading to switch it up a little.

- **You need to add a challenge to your program**, setting harder and harder goals, gradually over a period of time. Stick with the same challenge level for four to six weeks and then up your level. If you up your challenge level too quickly, your body will tell you. In this case, back off a bit to the previous challenge level and give it a few more weeks before ramping it up again. It's a real art, kind of like changing a diaper—*Just trust me on that one.*

Once you have your plan set up, start with something simple, and ease into a longer and harder routine. If you jump in too fast, you'll not only get exercise-induced injuries, but you'll get discouraged and quit before you even start. Start out with purposefully adding extra steps to your day by parking on the other end of the parking lot at Walmart. *My husband always does that. It used to drive me nuts, now I count it a blessing.* Take the stairs at work or at your apartment complex instead of riding the elevator. Add to that a ten to twenty-minute walk every day, and you've got your daily routine for your "on days."

The great news is that once you're pregnant, not only will you be able to continue exercising, but you'll be encouraged to do so! Healthy exercise is conducive to a healthy pregnancy, unless, of course, your doctor has to tell you to avoid strenuous activity.

WHEN TOO MUCH OF A GOOD THING IS BAD

Yes, exercising is good for you. Just like with your vitamins, though, you can get too much of a good thing! "How's that? Come again?!" That's right! In fact, getting too much exercise can even affect your fertility, keeping you from ovulating!

There's an easy way to know if your exercise routine is affecting your ovulation or not—track your monthly cycle. We'll be learning more about how to track your cycle and ovulation in the next section of the book, "Part Two: Stuffing the Sheets," but this part, today, is pretty easy. Each month, mark on your calendar when the first day your period was on and write on it which day you ovulated. *Do not write the words "ovulated" and "started period" on the calendar that hangs in the kitchen... Trust me when I say it can get kind of embarrassing the first time you have company over.*

119

Instead, circle the days in different colors. Red for the period day. A different color for the ovulation day. Count how many days it was from the day you ovulated until the day you started your period back. *I know. It seems kind of backward.* Mark these numbers on your calendar each month. Your period should come on day fourteen after ovulation. Heavy exercise can shorten this last half of your cycle. This is the first sign that your exercise regimen is too intense for your body. If this happens, it's crucial to immediately downsize your routine.

Symptoms of ovulation include:

- Lower abdominal pain or pelvic pain

- Possible spotting or discharge—Your discharge will be like egg whites.

- Increased sexual desire

- A change in basal temperature

- Breast tenderness

We'll talk more about knowing when you ovulate later. This will give you a pretty good idea, though, for charting purposes.

In this exercise section, the last thing I want to talk to you about is that you be sure to drink plenty of water. Your body needs 80 ounces (10 cups) of water every day. Spread it out throughout the day. There are times that you may need more water. These times include:

- When you exercise—*Surprise there...*

- When you pee a lot

- If you live in a climate that's hot and humid

- If you sweat a lot

- When you are vomiting and have diarrhea

Dehydration can happen in one day of battling a severe stomach flu without drinking enough fluids or taking in too little over a period of time. If you don't drink enough water and get dehydrated, your quality of life could be affected until you're hydrated again. You'll feel consistently fatigued, and your skin will be dry. Constipation and infrequent urination may worry you. Muscle cramps and *those stupid* kidney stones will make life difficult. You'll be continuously reaching for the mints or Winterfresh gum to wet your water-starved, dry mouth and to cover the bad breath dehydration causes. You could feel faint and weak. You might even have seizures or pass out. Be careful!

OVERCOMING BAD HABITS

There are many bad habits that we fall into as adults—and even as children, that carry over into adulthood. Some, we adopted because our parents had them when we were little, and we grew up believing that's what grown-ups do. We viewed them as a rite of adulthood. Some things stem from a lack of self-worth. We think we need to be like someone else to be worthy of their friendship, so we do something to earn their friendship—we partake in the drugs, alcohol, or our first cigarette. Others start merely as something to do. We're bored, wanting something new, adventure, the next best thing. We start with that bad habit and can't stop. What are some of the bad habits I'm referring to?

SMOKING

Out of all the pregnancy complications and all the threats to your baby-to-be, smoking is one of the most dangerous. In fact, Robert Welch, the chairman of the Department of Obstetrics and Gynecology at Providence Hospital in Southfield, MI, said that "smoking cigarettes is probably the number one cause of adverse outcomes for babies." He went on to say that it would be much safer and healthier for those babies if their mothers had a serious disease like high blood pressure or diabetes, which can be controlled with medications. "When a pregnant woman smokes," he said, "nothing can protect her baby from danger."

Dangers

"Why's it so dangerous?" *Glad you asked!*

Cigarettes contain over 4,000 chemicals, which includes lead, cyanide, over sixty compounds that cause cancer, and more. Would you pour a cocktail of cyanide and lead on your applesauce or strawberry yogurt and eat it? Well, you might as well be doing that when you smoke!

Not only is it unhealthy to you now, but it will be extremely unhealthy to you and your baby-to-be later when you're carrying your little "bun in the oven!" That brew of toxins, which makes its way into your bloodstream, will taint your veins, restricting them. Not only does this contaminate your future baby's only source of nutrients and oxygen, but it also limits the flow of that blood to him. Even just a few cigarettes a day can have horrible effects on your baby-to-be as he sits in your womb.

Partaking in even a few cigarettes a day can double the chances of premature birth. It also doubles the chances that your baby-to-be will be born at a weight of 5 ½ pounds or less. On top of that, sadly, it raises your chances by more than double for the risk that your baby will be stillborn.

We all know that smoking will affect our lungs when we smoke, but did you know it can affect your baby's as well? Not only would your baby be stuck on a respirator, unable to breathe on his own for a few days to a few weeks due to his (possible) small weight and size, his lungs may continue to develop slowly due to the nicotine in his body. He will have a much higher risk, by double or even triple the amount of other babies his age, of SIDS (sudden infant death syndrome). He will also be more vulnerable to asthma.

Two other good reasons to quit smoking now is because, if you smoke during pregnancy, your baby-to-be may be born with a very low IQ and have learning disorders or behavioral disorders. The second reason is that, if you smoke during the first three months of your pregnancy, your baby-to-be has a 20% to 70% higher chance of having a heart defect than that of those babies whose mothers didn't smoke during pregnancy.

Diligence

The best thing you can do for yourself and for your future baby-to-be is to diligently work on quitting those cigarettes while you're in the prepping stage. Not only is it bad for you and your baby, but it lowers your chances of getting pregnant by 40%! Also, if you quit now, you can focus more on being healthy, following that nutrition plan and exercise plan, instead of being distracted by trying to quit when you're trying to conceive or when you have that beautiful baby growing in your womb.

If you still find yourself smoking when you have that positive pregnancy test, don't worry yourself sick, just be diligent about quitting that first trimester! If you're able to quit during that first trimester, you raise the odds of having yourself a happy, healthy baby. If you quit in the second trimester of your pregnancy, you'll still increase your odds of delivering a full-term baby, but not by as much of a degree. For your health, for the health of your baby, for health's sake, stay diligent, and quit smoking during the prepping stage!

Helps

- **Quitting cold turkey** may be difficult, but it's the cheapest and safest way to quit at any stage of being a first-time mother, from prepping your body to holding that bundle of joy in your arms. Most people feel poorly for a few weeks while going through withdrawals, but you can do it! Approximately one out of twenty people are able to quit smoking that try to do it cold turkey. However, those who are prepping for pregnancy, trying to conceive, or already pregnant tend to beat those odds by a bit since their motivations are higher. If you use a nicotine replacement along with the quitting cold turkey method, your odds will also go up.

- **Quitting gradually** is a little easier but still difficult. Quitting gradually has the same odds of quitting as going cold turkey does. This step by step method does seem to work better than going cold turkey does when tackling this bad habit for those who are a pack a day-er or more. Quitting slowly may also help with the effects of withdrawal.

- **Nicotine replacement** is another avenue that may work for you. It's merely a replacement for the cigarettes, still offering the nicotine, which is the addictive element. It allows a step-down method, like the gradual method, without the prolongment of the toxins being pumped into your body. This method works for one in ten people, compared to the one in twenty of the gradual approach, but it can be expensive. It can run anywhere between $70 and $160 a month or more. This is much cheaper than many people spend on cigarettes a month. Nicotine replacement includes gum, patches, and nose sprays.

- **Bupropion (Zyban)** used to be sold as an antidepressant, called Wellbutrin. When doctors noticed that those taking Wellbutrin had an easy job at quitting smoking, they decided to research into the matter further. Not only does it avoid the use of nicotine, but it doesn't cause as much weight gain as other methods. *That gives it five stars in my book!* Bupropion, however, can cause seizures and is not recommended for those who are prone to seizures already. This medication costs approximately $130 per month. I say approximately since (1) prices change from pharmacy to pharmacy, and (2) your insurance may cover any part or all of the cost of any of the smoking cessation treatments listed.

- **Counseling** is basically talking to someone who can help you stay motivated and encouraged in what you're doing. This someone may offer you ideas in how to keep on keeping on and also on how to resist the temptation to have "just one cigarette," which of course turns into three and four, and, eventually, you're off the wagon completely. Just a few words of encouragement may be all it takes to keep you on the bandwagon! Motivation comes from within, but we need someone to build that up sometimes, to help us stay motivated. If no one is ready and forthcoming with words of encouragement when you need them, there are quitlines that you can call. A good, free one might be 1(800)QUIT-NOW or (800)784-8669. A private, professional counselor might run between $60 and $125 per session, while counseling with a group of others usually runs somewhere around $125 to $200 a class, which might last six to eight weeks. There is also Nicotine Anonymous and other free resources of the like.

- Lastly, there is **acupuncture or hypnosis**, which usually costs somewhere between $65 to $100 per session. Helping to calm those crazy cravings, they are safe approaches to quitting this bad habit. *You'll deal with lots of cravings once you get that precious "bun in the oven"! Hopefully not for cigarettes, but I totally understand the strength of cigarette cravings after pregnancy cravings gone wild!*

ALCOHOL

Another bad habit that must be overcome is drinking. Fetal alcohol syndrome is getting more and more common. You must start now at giving up alcohol. Doctors are adamant that alcohol must be abandoned altogether once a baby is conceived. No one has any idea what even a few drops of alcohol may have on your little baby-to-be as he develops in your womb.

Quitting habits that are unhealthy for you and will be unhealthy for your future baby-to-be can be hard. I understand that. Your doctors understand that. Talk to your doctor. Don't wait. He'll give you the tools to help you overcome your bad habits.

The most critical tool in quitting is to have someone to support you outside of your doctor, whether that be your spouse, your parents, or your best friend. It may even be a network of many people. They'll help you stay motivated. It's not an easy venture, but don't throw in the towel! Remember, there's a little future someone counting on you!

Chapter Seven: "College" Screenings

If you go into this thing full-speed ahead with lights flashing and sirens blaring, considering nothing but vitamins, minerals, nutrition, and exercise, it's like trying to study for exams without having ever set foot inside a classroom. There's so much more to it—things that must be considered, facts that, if known, will make life so much easier, and tests that must be run. First, let's prepare you for those "college course" tests you'll be administered during pregnancy by getting you graduated from "Prepping High" now. Later, after "Pregnancy College," of course, there's life after giving birth.

PRECONCEPTION CHECKUP

Before you become an official member of those prepping the bassinet, those trying to conceive their baby-to-be, you should get a preconception checkup. Most of the checkup will consist of the doctor asking you some questions. Don't worry. They won't be hard. We've already studied. I've already given you all the answers.

The first thing she'll want to get out of the way is making sure you're taking a prenatal vitamin with folic acid in it. If you've been listening, the answer will be yes. If not, get started now. You should be up and going on your prenatals a month before starting to try for conception.

She'll ask you about your diet and exercise routine. If you've read the previous chapter, "For Health's Sake," and have implemented any of the subjects I've covered, you'll be ready for these questions as well. Be careful to listen to any advice she has.

Your healthcare provider will also ask you about any bad habits you may have. These may include smoking, drinking, or drug use. These were covered in the previous chapter as well. If you need help quitting any of the above, you can call the Addiction and Alcohol Hotline at (844) 244-3171.

Next, she'll try to find out if you have any medical problems. She'll do this by asking you about your family history, doing bloodwork, and looking at your medical records. There are many different kinds of medical issues that must be well under control before you can safely become pregnant. She'll refer you to a specialist if necessary.

Your healthcare provider will go over your medications one by one, also reviewing your vitamins and minerals. Some medicines are not safe for you to take while you're pregnant. Some may even have a long half-life, which means they'll be stored in the body for a while even after the last dose is taken. These certain medications must be stopped weeks, sometimes even months, before you even start trying to conceive! Your doctor will start you on new, safer medications. You will not be left with no medicine at all.

She'll make sure you're immune to childhood diseases, like rubella and chickenpox. These can be detrimental in a pregnancy. Part of this is checking your records and checking directly with you to be sure your immunizations are up to date. She can also check to see if you are protected against some of these diseases and infections by running simple blood tests.

IMMUNIZATIONS

Because your immune system will be much lower when you're pregnant, you and your future baby-to-be, who will be snuggling safely in your womb when this becomes relevant, will need help fighting off certain illnesses and infections. What's the best and easiest way to do this without the toxicity of overdosing on vitamin C? Immunizations!

Doctors recommend getting most of your vaccinations before getting pregnant. In fact, there are only two they recommend during pregnancy. One is Tdap. This covers tetanus, diphtheria, and "Whooping Cough" (pertussis). The other vaccine is the influenza (Flu) vaccine.

Many babies less than six-months-old can contract Whooping Cough, some getting seriously ill and even dying from it. However, if you get your shot between 27 and 36 weeks along, it will help protect your baby by passing your antibodies on to him through the placenta. It will also keep you from getting sick. If you don't catch Whooping Cough, you can't pass it on to him after he's born.

The second and only other vaccine recommended during pregnancy is the flu vaccine. You see, during pregnancy, you re seven times more likely to contract a severe and even fatal case of it! Getting the Flu vaccination not only keeps you from the complications of severe dehydration and other complications, but it also prevents you from passing the Flu to your newborn and protects him from the Flu until he is 6-months-old.

There are several immunizations you cannot get during pregnancy due to their being made from live viruses. Because you should be protected against measles, rubella, polio, hepatitis B, tetanus, chickenpox, and the mumps during your pregnancy, you should get these immunizations at your Preconception Checkup. If you find you're pregnant before you get these immunizations, doctors agree that you should get them immediately following delivery.

These vaccinations are given for several reasons:

- **Chickenpox (varicella)**—If you catch this infection while you're pregnant, you and your baby can get severely ill. If you're not immunized or have never had chickenpox, you should get two doses of this shot. One dose of the vaccine only prevents 80-85% of cases, while two provide more protection. You should, then, wait at least four weeks before you start trying to conceive.

If you're not immune and *don't* get vaccinated, there's a small chance your baby could get Congenital Varicella syndrome if you contract the virus. The risk of this is the highest when you are between 13 and 20 weeks along. This syndrome can cause birth defects, like malformed limbs, scarring on his skin, and neurological problems. Your baby may be born with an abnormally small head and vision problems. A baby whose mother contracted chickenpox during pregnancy has the chance of suffering seizures and not growing well while in the womb. Congenital Varicella may also cause mental or physical developmental disabilities. There's also a higher risk of miscarriage or stillbirth.

If you do come down with chickenpox during your pregnancy, your doctor will suggest you get a detailed ultrasound. In this ultrasound, he will check for problems, such as signs of defects. At least one more ultrasound will follow. You'll also be given the option to speak with a maternal-fetal medicine specialist or genetic counselor to talk about the risks you and your baby may face.

- **Measles, mumps, and rubella (MMR)**—Some studies have shown reason for concern that there may be a link between measles and mumps and miscarriage. These may also raise the risk of birth defects, but this hasn't been proven. Rubella, however, is responsible for several severe birth defects. These include eye problems, intellectual disability, deafness, and heart defects. If you were born after 1966, be sure to talk to your doctor about getting a booster vaccination. This will give you full protection against all three.

- **Pneumococcal**—If you're a smoker or have a lung or kidney disease, chronic heart disease, or diabetes, you will need a pneumococcal vaccine. This disease causes serious illness including pneumonia, meningitis, or a bloodstream infection (sepsis).

Pneumonia can cause many complications during pregnancy if left untreated or if it develops into a severe case, which it can do quickly. Your oxygen levels may drop, unable to send enough oxygen to the rest of your body. You may develop empyema, a condition in which you get "water on your lungs" (this is a term that refers to fluids filling your lungs by any amount). The infection in your lungs can also spread out of your lungs and into other parts of your body. If left untreated, both you and your baby could die.

Pneumonia can also affect your baby. Some of these complications may include low birth weight, respiratory failure, premature birth, and miscarriage.

- **Travel vaccinations**—Travel to some countries requires the traveler to receive certain vaccines. Many of these vaccines, however, are unsafe to receive during pregnancy. If you plan to travel anytime in the few years following your preconception checkup (you never know how long it'll take you to get pregnant), you should get the following vaccines during it. By the way, many of these vaccines take four weeks to become fully effective, so it's recommended that you not travel for at least that long following the immunizations. The recommended vaccinations vary depending on which country you're traveling to, but some of them may include the:

- o   Varicella vaccine

- o   Adult diphtheria and tetanus vaccine

- o   Oral polio vaccine (OPV)

- o   Hepatitis A vaccine

- o   Hepatitis B vaccine

- o   Meningococcal vaccine

- o   Typhoid vaccine

- o   Japanese encephalitis vaccine

- o   Rabies vaccine

- o   Yellow fever (YF) vaccine

**The last thing I want to talk to you about under travel immunizations is malaria prevention. I know this isn't necessarily an immunization, but it is something you have to watch out for if you go overseas.

Not only is it easier for you to get malaria when you're pregnant, but it's another one of those infections that are more severe when you're carrying a baby than when you're not. Malaria can also bring with it serious complications for your baby. Just as every immunization is not safe for you while you're carrying your little one in your womb, neither are all anti-malarial medications. You'll definitely want to discuss your trip with your healthcare provider beforehand. Most of all, be careful to adequately prepare!

SEXUALLY TRANSMITTED DISEASES

Another thing you can expect during your preconception checkup is a pelvic exam and Pap smear. *I know. I know. You probably cringed right there. I did too.* This is usually only done if you haven't had a "lady checkup" in at least a year.

If you or you're partner are sexually active with another person or have been in the past, you may be at risk for a sexually transmitted disease. It's very possible to have a sexually transmitted disease, or sexually transmitted infection, (STI) without any symptoms at all. If you choose, you will be tested for these. For your safety, the safety of others, and the safety of your future baby-to-be, you *should* get tested. This'll happen during your preconception checkup or, if you miss doing this then, you can have this test done on your first prenatal checkup.

Will the Diseases Hurt My Baby?

"I know STIs affect me," you might say, "but how will they affect my baby-to-be?"—It's so important to find out if you have an STI now, before you're pregnant, and jump on treating it! If you leave these untreated, many things can happen to your baby as a result of the different STIs during your pregnancy. Let's explore some of the STIs and the possible effects:

- **Hepatitis B**—Approximately 90% of mothers who have acute hepatitis B will pass it on to their babies. Of those mothers with a chronic case of hepatitis B, about 10-20% will pass it to their baby. However, transmission of this infection can be thwarted if your baby is treated as soon as possible after delivery. An infected newborn who has not been treated, or whose treatment did not work, has up to a 90% chance that he will become a carrier himself. Being a carrier means others will be able to contract the virus from him. He will have a chronic infection, carrying it for the rest of his life. As an adult, there's a 25% probability that he'll die from liver cancer or cirrhosis of the liver.

- **Hepatitis C**—Not only can your baby contract this infection, but it can cause other problems as well. For instance, your baby could be born with low birth weight and have small gestational size throughout. He's also at risk of being born prematurely.

- **Gonorrhea**—As with the other two STIs, Gonorrhea can be passed to your baby. If it's not treated adequately with antibiotics beforehand, which can effectively cure it, it can cause your membranes to rupture prematurely, premature birth, and low birthweight. A baby who contracts gonorrhea during birth can also get an eye infection, which can lead to blindness. These eye infections can be prevented with the medication given to every baby upon delivery. There are also blood infections, which could be deadly, and joint infections that could plague your baby.

- **Syphilis**—If you have Syphilis, it's not something you want to deal with during pregnancy. It can cause rupture of the membranes, premature birth, and low birth weight. It can also cause your baby to die after birth. You see, babies who haven't been treated have a higher risk of having problems with several of their organs.

- **Chlamydia**—Here's another one that can cause your membranes to rupture prematurely. It can also cause you to go into preterm labor and cause your baby to have a low birth weight. This STI can also be transmitted during vaginal birth. This is another that can be treated successfully with antibiotics if it's diagnosed and treated while you're pregnant. However, it must be caught, which means you must be tested!

- **HIV**—It's also important to find if you have HIV before you get pregnant or, at least, in early pregnancy. It's possible to reduce the risk of passing it on to your precious baby-to-be. Pregnant women can pass HIV to their babies during pregnancy, labor, and vaginal delivery, or breastfeeding.

However, if HIV is diagnosed before or early in pregnancy, steps can be taken to reduce the risk of transmission. For instance, you can have a scheduled cesarean. You can take HIV medications while you're carrying your baby and during his delivery. Also, after he's born, your baby can take 4 to 6 weeks of HIV medications to help his little body resist any risk of infection from any HIV he may have been exposed to. If the test confirms that you have HIV and you start HIV meds immediately and take them through pregnancy, and if your baby takes his HIV medicine for the 4 to 6 weeks following birth, his risk of contracting the virus can be lowered all the way down to 2% or less! A few similar steps can be taken for other viral infections as well.

**I'll throw this in for free!* If you're infected with HIV, you should not breastfeed your baby either. Your baby can contract the infection through your breastmilk. There are plenty of healthy and safe formulas out there. I know this may be heartbreaking to some of you, but it's for your baby's good.

There are also other types of STIs out there. The effects of these can be:

- Pneumonia

- Brain damage

- Eye infection

- Chronic liver disease

- Blindness

- Blood infection

- Deafness

Preventing new STIs while you're pregnant is very important. I've convinced you (*I hope*) that testing for a current STI is necessary, but what if you contract one during pregnancy? What do you do then? How do you know? What if you don't know and your baby gets infected? What if your baby is born with an STI, extreme malformations or other birth defects, or is born dead or miscarried? How do you fix this before it starts? What can you do?

*What **Do** I Do?*

This one is simple!

"Really!?" you might blurt out, half in excitement, half in unbelief. "How do I keep my future baby-to-be safe? How do I keep **myself** safe so I *can* keep my baby safe? I mean, can't you get AIDs from anywhere? I heard you can even get it from changing an infected baby's diaper! I work at a daycare... And what about herpes? Can't you get that from a public toilet seat?"

Whoa! Slow down, there, Sweets! First, let's go over some common myths. One that you were worried about above had to do with toilet seats. The term "sexually transmitted disease" or "sexually transmitted infection" means that it's sexually transmitted. Unless you're having sex with the toilet seat, you can't get an STI from it. There *is* a slight-slight possibility that you might have some pubic lice jump on you, but that's very unlikely unless the toilet is putrid.

STIs don't live in urine but do be careful to wipe it off the seat before sitting down. *I mean, gross!* Also, make sure that "if *you* sprinkle when you tinkle, to be a sweetie and wipe the seatie!" You don't want others to have to do it!

Now, let's get on to those myths that you may not currently think about, but that may pop up in the future. These myths need to be covered now so they'll be there for easy access when you come to that point when you're trying to conceive or when you're pregnant with your precious baby. Also, if they're listed now, they'll be here for easy reference later. The myth will be listed first. The fact will be listed afterward in bold. I'll also include the "What to Do" under the term, *"For Safety's Sake,"* to keep yourself (and your future baby-to-be) safe.

- MYTH #1—If one female performs with another woman, neither will contract an STI.

FACT #1—You can still contract any STIs the other woman has. Oral sex can spread STI's as can sex toys. You can contract STIs through the exchange of the vaginal fluids swapped on them. These infections can also be transmitted through contact of skin on skin.

For Safety's Sake—The best way to prevent an STI is abstinence. Obviously, if you're planning to have a baby in the future, this would be an impossible feat. However, because the best way to prevent STI's when you DO need a relationship with a man to get that baby in your belly, a monogamous relationship is the safest way to stay "safe." To keep your future bundle of joy safe, stay away from other relationships, despite any temptation, and stick with your one and only.

- MYTH #2—People don't need to worry about it with their new partner! People with STIs display certain symptoms. Those visual symptoms show if they carry any STIs and if they will, therefore, infect others with anything.

FACT #2—STIs don't always show symptoms at all in the early stages. In fact, that's why it's important you get tested in your preconception checkup! You may not have any symptoms and think you're just fine. Your partner may believe the same thing. Just because they *look* alright doesn't mean they *are* alright. Your partner can infect you (and vice-versa by the way) without even knowing they're infected themselves, and you will be putting your future baby-to-be at risk.

For Safety's Sake—*Before that "first time" with your new partner, you should both undergo testing. You for his and your baby-to-be's sake, and him for your sake and, ultimately, for what will become his future baby as well.*

- MYTH #3—When couples have already had unprotected sex once, it doesn't matter anymore. They can continue to have unprotected sex because both partners are now infected anyway.

FACT #3—Even if you've already "done the deed" once, you may not yet be infected. Besides, even if you are, what if he has other STIs he's not aware of or another strain of the same STI? The two of you could also pass the infection back and forth between each other if both of you are not treated simultaneously.

For Safety's Sake—The correct and consistent use of LATEX condoms and LATEX dental dams will protect you until you can both be treated. They must be latex since natural membrane-based condoms don't prevent STIs as effectively. Also, if you must use a lubricant, which certainly makes things more comfortable, DO NOT use those that are oil-based. Oil-based lubricants will degrade and weaken the condom.

- MYTH #4—If both partners take a hot shower before sex, carefully scrubbing each area well, neither partner can pass their infection to the other.

FACT #4—Although good hygiene may help cut down on the possibility of any urinary tract infections, it will not keep you from contracting an STI.

For Safety's Sake--You shouldn't "wash" afterward by way of douching either. Not only is it never a good idea for any woman since it throws off the balance of the vaginal flora, but douching after sex may force any sexually transmitted infection higher up inside, thus affecting the reproductive organs.

- MYTH #5—A woman's monthly contraceptive pill, IUD, or other birth control will offer her protection against STIs.

FACT #5—The only birth control that can possibly offer any protection at all against STIs is condoms, and even those aren't 100% reliable. That's typically due to user error.

*For Safety's Sake—Learn the proper use and wear of a condom, whether you be using a female condom or a male. The first thing you need to do with a male condom is to check the expiration date (and you'll want to do this before the foreplay starts). If it's expired, it's a NO! Second, make sure there's an air bubble in the package, which ensures that the condom hasn't been damaged. Next, make sure the condom is right side out and place it on him **as soon as his man part stands at attention,** unrolling the condom all the way to the top. Lastly, at the end of your "fun," have him hold onto the condom before withdrawal. If the condom does accidentally get left behind, twist the end before you remove it to prevent any leaks.*

- MYTH #6—The infection won't be spread to his partner if the male pulls out before he ejaculates.

FACT #6—You can get infected or even pregnant from pre-cum, which is the fluid your partner secretes while you are initiating foreplay.

For Safety's Sake-- The best way to use a condom is to make it part of the foreplay rather than a distraction or pause in the middle of sex, and you want to put it on your man as soon as he erects so that there doesn't end up being any uh-ohs along the way.

- MYTH #7—As long as two people stick with each other only and have for years, neither need to be tested for STIs because there's no way either could have one or get one.

FACT #7—What if your partner had a relationship with another woman before you came along? Maybe you have an open relationship, and he told you about the prior relationship. Perhaps he didn't tell you for fear of hurting you even though it was long before he ever met you. Either way, what if that woman had an STI? What if your husband or boyfriend doesn't even know, has shown no symptoms, and simply has

never been told? You could be infected and not have a clue even though you have only ever had one partner.

For Safety's Sake—I think the questions I asked in the "FACT #7" section are sufficient to spawn enough though for the "For Safety's Sake" section. You just never really know who has what. As I said before, both of you should get tested. If you test positive, get treated simultaneously. After you've both been given the free and clear, whether it be due to the treatment or both of you having tested negative (YAY!!), stay with your uninfected monogamous partner.

- <u>MYTH #8</u>—If two people don't have penetrative sex, but only mess around with foreplay and oral sex, they cannot contract the other's STIs.

FACT #8—If you have oral sex, you could be infected with herpes or other STIs. Herpes, crabs, and scabies can even be spread through the simple act of a kiss—*okay… tonsil hockey, ladies,* or even by just sleeping in the same bed! If your partner is infected with HPV, it could spread to you if your genitals rub together or if you engage in mutual masturbation.

For Safety's Sake—I know this is going to seem simple to some of you and abominable to others, but, honestly, what would you tell your daughter if she were faced with the same circumstances? My suggestion, in this case, is to keep your clothes on! It's the easiest way to keep from moving on to oral sex. It's the easiest way to keep your genitals from rubbing together. It's the easiest way to keep intimate skin from touching skin. It's the easiest way to keep from contracting an STI. If you're going to have penetrative sex, get yourselves tested. While you're waiting, wear a condom. If you're keeping yourself for the wedding day, (and, if you are, YOU'RE AWESOME!), for safety's sake, just keep those clothes on.

Lastly, don't forget, you can spread STI's to him as well. Remember, I said that STIs are a silent infection and that you can have it without even knowing? For your sake, for the sake of your partner, but mostly for the sake of your future baby-to-be, GET TESTED!!

"COLLEGE" SCREENINGS

Another part of your preconception checkup consists of your healthcare provider's recommendation for you and your partner to have "genetic carrier screening" done. If we consider pregnancy as "College," this is the screenings to see if you still want to go through with the admittance exam. You'll see why in a moment. Genetic carrier screening is merely a set of tests that are done to determine what, if any, serious inherited illnesses you and/or your spouse or boyfriend may carry in your genes. Some of the over one-hundred diseases that might be tested for and caught are sickle cell disease, Tay-Sachs disease, thalassemia, and cystic fibrosis. If both of you carry one gene for the same disorder for, say, sickle cell disease, your baby-to-be will have a 25% possibility of inheriting a gene from you both and, therefore, having that disease.

Will it Break the Bank?

The screening isn't costly and is worth every penny. It used to be quite expensive, but the price has dropped a lot over the years as technology has developed. Now that genetic carrier screening is strongly suggested as part of your preconception checkup, some insurance companies cover it (**I'll throw this in for free too*—It's also considered part of your prenatal care if a preconception

153

checkup was forgotten or not known about. I had four kiddos and never knew anything about preconception checkups). Some insurance companies see the carrier screenings as optional and will not cover it. However, even in such a case, these screenings usually cost less than a few hundred dollars.

How's it Done?

It's not a hard test, a twenty-page paper you have to fill out, or a marathon you have to run. No, all you have to do is give a blood or saliva sample. If you test positive as a carrier, they'll test the future father-to-be as well. Sometimes, if you opt to, they can test you both at the same time to speed up the process a little.

You can go with the "traditional" screening or the "expanded" carrier training. In the traditional testing, you're only tested for the common mutations that your baby-to-be might be at risk for. For instance, if a family member of either future parent has a family member with a particular disorder or is a genetic carrier of a disorder, or if either future parent is part of a specific race that might have a higher chance of getting a particular disease, that disease will be tested for.

There's a problem with that, though. So many Americans don't know what nationalities they come from! Do you know what all races you have in you? I don't. I know I have German, French, English, a few Native American tribes, and... maybe a few other things? If I were a puppy dog, they'd call me a mutt. My mom always called us kiddos a "Heinz 57" variety. Another problem is that many people these days are adopted or don't know who their daddy is. Therefore, there are many of us, who have no idea what our ethnic background is!

If you are one of us Heinz 57 varieties or if you're among those blessed to have been adopted, you might want to take the option for the expanded carrier screening. This test screens for a much more expanded array of disease mutations. It tests for all of them (over one-hundred) rather than the very few the traditional screening offers. If this screening isn't offered to you, you can always ask for it. Now's not the time to be shy.

DECISIONS, DECISIONS!

Genetic screening in your preconception period, or even in early pregnancy, has several advantages. The most significant of these is that you can know, before birth, that your baby may need special treatment starting at birth or soon after. You'll have the ability to have the necessary specialists all lined up and ready to go so they can start treating him directly after delivery.

Being that you were offered the screenings before you became pregnant with your precious bundle, you will have plenty of options before you. Your doctor should point you toward a genetic counselor if you both test as carriers for the same gene. A genetic counselor will be able to assist you, informing you of your possibilities.

- One possible choice, if you decide to skip having your own baby as planned or simply choosing to wait until later to have your own, is adoption. Some people adopt babies. Others adopt young children, older children, or teens. However, they will be no less your children and make you no less their mother than if you had stuck with your original plan. Many people foster children and end up adopting them because "they work their way into your heart in a way that seems impossible," I've been told. I have friends that have adopted children. They said they feel closer to them than they ever could have a biological child.

- Another way to become the mother you want to be is through artificial insemination. This is where a sperm donor, who is not a carrier, donates his sperm to implant into your egg so you can have a happy, healthy baby. You should make certain your partner is 100% on-board with this before moving forward.

- Knowing your risks, you might decide to go on with your plan for conception and pregnancy. The genetic counselor can help you be ready for the medical circumstances and possible disabilities that may follow. I understand it would be heartbreaking to be forced to take another route other than which you'd planned—unaided pregnancy. Just remember that there is that 1 in 4 chance that your baby may be born with that genetic disease. This is where the genetic counselor comes in.

In this case, you might want to think about calling upon a medical geneticist as one of the specialists in your corner. A medical geneticist is a doctor that's board certified in the field of genetics and specially trained in that area. If you decide to look into adding a medical geneticist to the list of your baby-to-be's group of specialists, ready to treat your baby if you find he is born with the disease you and your partner carry, there is an online tool that can be consulted for finding genetic services. You can find it upon doing an internet search for "The American College of Medical Genetics and Genomics."

*****

PART TWO

STUFFING THE SHEETS

*****

Chapter One: Getting to Know Your Body

After you've done everything you can to prepare your body for conceiving your baby, it's time to stuff those sheets full of you and your partner and try to have your baby. The very first thing you should do, though is to get to know your body. If you're coming at this thing as a virgin, there's a lot for you to learn!

Tips for Newlyweds

My husband and I, as newlyweds, learned much of this the hard way. We had both kept ourselves until our wedding day, and no one had ever set us down and told us how to do things properly. That's what we're going to talk about first. I suggest sitting down and going over these points with your husband together and maybe even Googling more or getting a good book on the subject.

- First, Relax together beforehand (unless it's a spontaneous thing). Read a book, take a bath, listen to music, whatever works for the two of you. This will calm both of your nerves, relax your body, and make life

160

so much easier for you. **By the way, you really need to relax anyway. Relaxing helps to melt away stress. Stress can cause your body to fail to ovulate, which means, no baby for another month!*

- You may be self-conscious about your body, which you must express to your husband. He can slow down his advances or wait until a later time. Be open with him. It'll make him feel good to know you love him and trust him enough to tell him the truth about how you feel. If you've never shown anyone your naked body before, it can be a little daunting. That's okay, and he'll understand. In fact, he may feel the same exact way.

- It takes a lot of foreplay before a woman is ready for sex. Your partner might be immediately ready, but your body does not work like that. Someone once told me (after we went on our honeymoon—*a lot of good that did*) that men are like a kettle, ready at a moment's notice, while a woman's body is more like a crockpot, which has to cook all day long before it is prepared for sexual intimacy. You might try prolonged kissing, fondling, oral sex, and even small things like full-body massages or role play leading up to penetration.

- Lubricant is your friend—lots and lots of lubricant! When you're self-conscious or nervous, or when things are just all new, it may make it so you're unable to produce the natural juices you need to have comfortable relations. You want to get where you can have sex, eventually, with just your natural lubricant (lots of foreplay will allow your body to create this with time). Certain types of lubricant can actually hinder the sperm from reaching your egg, keeping many of them trapped in the lubricant.

- Lastly, sex might be uncomfortable the first time. I've heard of some people it was for and some that had no trouble. It was for me the first few times we tried because I was so dry. We didn't know to use lubricant or foreplay—like I said, we were talked to about those things AFTER our honeymoon. *Notice I said "tried," by the way. My husband didn't go any further once I said something. We didn't actually succeed at sex until after our honeymoon.* I was one that had no trouble after the talk, but my husband was very gentle and took things very slowly. I'm not certain if that made a difference or not. Speak to your husband on this matter. Remind him of this possibility and of the methods that can be used to avoid hurting you. He doesn't want to hurt you in any

162

way. Take your time. Use a lot of foreplay. "Warm up that crockpot." Make sure your well lubricated, then move slowly, and you should be fine.

- Oh! One last thing! I'm going to tell you something that my grandmother told me, something I find wise now that I have four children and a few years behind me. You and your husband might consider taking a year or two to get to know each other really well before starting a little family. You need some time alone to just be with one another and learn how to become a family of two before you ever become a family of three.

THE WONDERS OF IT ALL

Yes, it feels terrific, but more than that, it is a deep showing of great love, a giving of oneself to another. Sex is a sacred union between two people and not something to be taken lightly. But why does it feel so good? Does it *always* feel good? What if it doesn't? What if it hurts? Does that mean it's just not for you? Does that mean you're doomed to a hell of the duty of sex in marriage and *having* to have sex if you want a baby? What can you do? God tells us sex inside marriage is a wonderful and beautiful thing. Why would He lie? Let me tell you how to make it wonderful, how to make your body comply. Let me tell you how to get in touch with your body. It's important to really know your body before you can experience the wonders of sex.

PREPARE YOUR LIBIDO

As I mentioned above, your body needs to steep all day long, like sun tea in a jar, to be ready at night. Get yourself in a frisky mindset. You don't want sex to merely be a simple afterthought at the day's end, and you don't want it to be something that rules your mind all day long. I mean it'd be kind of weird to be thinking of sex with your partner while you're discussing the latest rise of the DOW with your boss in the office. There must be a balance. I think about my husband and his awesomeness and sexiness on and off all day and then concentrate on it off and on all evening, imagining him shirtless. I make a point to touch him, flirt with him, and talk to him all evening. Before children, we used to draw the blinds and dim the lights in the evening, and I would cook and serve dinner in my lingerie and sit in his lap to eat. This definitely set my mood and prepared my body and mind for sex. It definitely had him looking forward to life after dinner too.

Nowadays, even with four kids, I have my ways of having that sex-feeling all day long. While home, I wear loose fitting pants and a big shirt without undergarments and then switch into a robe after the kids go to bed with absolutely nothing underneath, my husband being privy of each (the first while he's at work all day—*hee hee*).

PREPARE YOUR BODY

There are a number of things you can do to prepare yourself for sex, and one of them is preparing your body. "What do you mean?" Well, how sexy do you feel with a forest growing on your legs? Here are some ideas:

- Shave your legs.

- Do your hair.

- Put on makeup.

- Clip and paint your nails—don't forget those toenails!

- Put on jewelry.

- Take a shower.

- Put on sexy undergarments.

PREPARE YOUR MIND

You want to be rejuvenated and ready to go when your partner is. There are some ways to prepare yourself so you are. The biggest helper to rejuvenation is not coffee or tea, but simple rest. Set aside a time to take a nap or sit in your recliner and just veg. You must rest if you want to be at the top of your game. If you're anything like me, you go from sunup to sundown with hardly any thought for self in between. Take a short rest!

Make some time for yourself. Read a book or play a game—maybe on your phone or computer or play sudoku or something of the sort. Take a bubble bath. *You can even use a rubber duckie if you want! I promise not to tell.* Set this time apart, or it will never happen!

Set a routine. You would not believe how much this calms your mind, organizing it, preparing it for anything that might lie ahead. It gives you the ability to control your life in such a way that you won't feel rushed during the whole time you're making love.

EXPLORING THE WONDERS OF YOU

Many couples don't know the secret to good marital relations. They merely have sex as a duty to one another or as an avenue toward the goal of having a baby. The man usually has no problems when sex is just jumped right into. He's ready all the time. However, a woman is built differently. "So what's that secret?" Your partner needs to take the time to explore the wonders that are you. Your body craves this.

LET'S FOCUS ON FOREPLAY

Foreplay is any sexual touching that comes before sex. It's a part of intimacy that your body needs in order to enjoy sex fully. My husband's and my foreplay begins as part of our clothing removal, with our hands traveling to the far reaches of Neverland, and continues from there.

Foreplay should never stand off alone on its own, and neither should sex. It should all be one intimate experience from the warm-up during the day/ "crockpot time" to the cool-off and clean-up time afterward. In fact, as part of the experience, it'll make the sex experience more... well... let's just say you'll experience ground-shaking fireworks. The more time and effort you give to the foreplay portion of the experience, the more intense "it" will be!

You'll also find that both of you must be involved to make it enjoyable. If you're not ready for foreplay, "dress up" in your lingerie and take some more time to talk or play games or snuggle. Take some more time to tell those intimate stories to one another. Play a "Do you remember..." game from recent memories of sexual experiences. Read a romantic book together. Read this part of this book together.

JUST TELL HIM!

MOST IMPORTANT!! COMMUNICATE!!! Men like you to be rough with them, but your body needs them to be gentle with you—*newsflash!* Many women feel discomfort and sometimes even pain when touched roughly—especially in their "no-zones." We're not built the same way. We're like fine china and meant to be handled as such, not only in bed, but always.

I always tell my kids, even, " You have to be gentle with Mommy. I'm breakable!" They're so rambunctious during the day. Children don't mean to be rough and tough and tumbly. They just are. That includes when they're jumping into your lap elbows and knees first.

The same is true with your husband in the bed. Communicate. Tell him when he's too rough. He doesn't mean to hurt you. He just doesn't know. He thinks you like the same he does. He doesn't remember or realize you're different than he is, that God made you different. Tell him, and then remind him often because he'll forget, "Honey, be gentle. I'm breakable."

Another part of communication is to make sure not to leave him hanging. Don't just tell him what you don't like (roughness) and leave it there. Tell him what you do like! Be personal! Tell him where and how you want to be touched. "Rougher, gentler. Up, down. Side to side, circular. More, less." My husband loves that, and I'm sure your's will too!

DON'T FORGET HIM!

In the process of intimate foreplay, in the intimate touching, it's easy to forget to touch your partner intimately, to return the favor. It's just as fun for you to pleasure him as it is for him to pleasure you!

169

Have fun with it! Torment him! Tease him! Take your clothes off in front of him… very slowly… Maybe put on some music and role play a stripper. Maybe have some sexy lingerie hidden beneath your clothes—this would help you get your mind and body ready too! Be creative. The idea is to get his mouth watering, his eyes wandering, and his mind wondering.

Rub his body. Remember, men like it rougher than women do! Ask him if he wants you to be gentler or rougher, if you're in the right places, and exactly what he wants. Wander around certain spots before you finally move in and begin stimulating him. You have a power over him you never realized. Your body can do amazing things. Get to know it!

YOUR BODY'S EXPRESSIONS

How do you have an orgasm? What is an orgasm? Have you ever had one? All of these are important questions. An orgasm is both physically and emotionally related. It's a wonderful sensation that starts in your toes and travels up your body, making your vaginal muscles tighten, which pulls the sperm into the uterus, as you reach a climax during sex. It doesn't have to come through penetration but came come through certain types of foreplay as well. According to ABC News, only 25% of women ever reach this mind-blowing climax from only sexual penetration alone. Of that 75 % who need help to achieve an orgasm outside of sexual penetration, 10 to 15% *never* orgasm.

You may feel selfish doing so—I used to, but you must focus on what's happening in *your* body if you're going to climax. Focus on the feelings inside your body and out. Focus on the man causing the sensations. Focus on the warmth of your partner's skin under your hands or his hair between your fingers if his head happens to be between your legs during a part of your foreplay. Focus on his smell, the sounds of his breathing and yours, the sight of his body—even the parts you may not be able to see. Your body needs this if you're going to orgasm.

YOU'VE GOT THE NERVE!

Your body is made up of bones and cartilage, muscles, organs, which includes your skin and brain, and it's made up of your nerves. One place in your body that has lots of nerves is your vagina. There are two special spots in your vagina that contain lots of nerve endings called the clitoris and the G-spot. The clitoris is near the front, top of your vagina, above the urethra while the G-spot is on the inside, also on the top toward the pelvic bone. You

171

can tell your man to feel for the spot that feels like it has a different texture. The G-spot will create a more intense orgasm.

CHANGE IT UP

If you're not finding sex satisfying, maybe you need to change your position so your partner will be rubbing your clitoris and G-spot as you have intercourse.

"How?" you might ask.

Well, if you're one of those that just lie there, you will not be stimulated much at all, if any. However, if you tilt your pelvis toward your partner, his penis will be able to rub both of your nerve-filled areas! This will arouse your pleasure center like you wouldn't believe, especially if you kiss and let your hands roam at the same time. Your body needs all your senses engaged during sex.

Try motion. Rock your hips, thrusting when he does. This gives you even more stimulation. Doing Kegels when he's on his way out not only brings him pleasure but will add to yours as well.

Another position you might try is being on top. Have your partner lie down on his back and have some fun. I sometimes start out with this as part of our foreplay when I'm feeling frisky and want to give him some extra pleasure. Not only does he not have to work for what he's getting, but you can change your angle anytime you want and in any way you need to make sure those spots get hit.

Knowing your body, the way it functions, and the way sex feels may not be vital to conceiving a baby, but it'll help. Does this mean you *have* to orgasm to get pregnant? NO! Remember the statistics from the beginning? Ten to fifteen percent of women never experience an orgasm, and 75% of woman cannot orgasm with their man inside of them, but only with outside help. They have to have sex toys, oral sex, or hand stimulation. Well, many of those get pregnant! In fact, I never orgasmed without of outside stimulation until a few years ago, and I have four children!

Knowing the secrets to sex, such as relaxing, lubrication, and foreplay will get your man inside, newlyweds. Remember, it's not just the physical side of your body that needs attention, ladies. Your mind needs to be prepped by readying your psyche and your physical appearance. You must rejuvenate your body through rest. Foreplay will, not only make your juices flow, readying your body for sex, but will also make the whole experience more pleasurable. Don't forget to tell your partner if you need him to move up or down or all around. Let him know if he needs to push harder or back off a bit.

An orgasm during foreplay can excite your body enough that, even if you don't typically have an orgasm with your husband inside, you might. Communicate with your spouse. Tell him if you need him to slow down during sex or speed up, to hump harder or be gentler. You'll know what your body needs to lead to orgasm. Listen to it! An orgasm causes a suction, pulling the sperm up into your uterus. Like I said, it isn't necessary for pregnancy, but it couldn't hurt. Get to know your body.

CHAPTER TWO: POSITIONALLY INCORRECT

So, you've been having orgasm after orgasm, and you still got your period this month? Stop worrying so much! It's normal for it to take a while. It's not an overnight thing. *By the way—breaking news! Neither is pregnancy and delivery.* Conception takes most people *much* longer than a month. These are the hard, cold facts, ladies, but there is so much fiction out there to wade through as well. Many people hold a position that's incorrect, and you may be one of them! Let's find out if you are.

YOUR POSITION

Some people swear up and down that *your* position makes a difference, that you must lay certain ways to increase the odds of pregnancy. **They're the ones that are positionally incorrect.** When it comes to the "best position" for conceiving, well, that's all up in the air.

Scientist can't really say whether one position's better for conception or not, but this one thing we know, one certain position isn't the best for everyone. You can see where it might be pretty hard to scientifically study the different sexual positions and the fertility results due to the differences in everyone's build, fertility status, and more. Every one of us is built differently—and so are our men. Finding any two sets of people (never mind two sets of people for every position) that meet the same exact criteria and are willing to go through the... *um*... scrutiny necessary for the test would be nigh impossible. Even then, the builds, the level of fertility on both partners, uterus and cervix design, separate conditions or medical elements, and more have an effect on which position might work best for one person or the other.

MISSIONARY POSITION

Some studies have hinted this position may offer a small advantage. With you laying on your back, your cervix is in a position to receive your partner's sperm more readily. Some also think the little swimmers *may possibly* get trapped in the cervical mucus more readily in this position.

This *may* be advantageous for the near 66% of women whose uterus is tipped forward as it should be, but what about the other 34%? We are informed by a professor of reproductive biology and psychiatry at Case Western Reserve University School of Medicine and the chief of the Division of Behavioral Medicine at University Hospitals Case Medicine Center, Sheryl A Kingsberg, that the missionary position isn't advantageous to these women at all.

Not only do you not know if your uterus is tipped forward or backward to know if this position may *possibly* help you conceive or not, but it may also cause your partner pain. Because men have to use all their muscles to perform in the missionary position, putting their full weight on their arms and knees, it's taxing on them. Clinical psychologist and sex therapist at New York University's Fertility Center and in private practice, Mindy R. Schiffman, Ph. D., confirms this.

COWGIRL POSITION

The cowgirl position has to do with you being mounted on top of your man. Though this can be beneficial in that you can face your partner, control how deep he goes, and can control how fast the thrusting happens, it can also be tiring for you. Not only that but, even though your man may really like it, it's one of the leading causes in penile fractures today.

Those that tell you this position will hinder your efforts toward pregnancy are *half* right, you know. Sitting on top while you "do it" may have a negative effect. Don't forget, your partner's little men do have to fight a little to get upstream to meet their forever home, and gravity pulling them the opposite direction can't be a good thing. A man's ejaculation, however, is quite far. The stream shoots seven to ten inches on average, in fact, far enough to get the semen up to the cervix and stuck in your thinned out cervical mucus. That sperm-laden mucus will then be drawn up into the uterus during your orgasm, should you have one, or it will swim up there on its own using the mucus to glide on through.

LADY'S CHOICE

Honestly, the best position is whatever position is best for you. Good news! You choose! *Yay!* The important thing is that you consistently have relations frequently from a few days after your period until a few days after you ovulate. Charting will help. We'll talk about how to chart for conception and all those fun things in the next chapter.

UNUSUAL POSITIONS

The director of the infertility service at Cleveland Clinic, Dr. James Goldfarb, told WebMD something that I found informational. He said that sometimes, though very rarely, if your cervix is in certain, unusual positions, then a particular sex position with your partner *can* make a difference.

About one-quarter of all women worldwide have an unusually positioned cervix, called a tilted cervix. A typical cervix lies in a straight line, in front of the bladder. A tilted cervix is somewhat anterior to the pelvis. Though it used to be held to cause infertility, we now know that this doesn't make it any harder for a woman to conceive at all. *I can vouch for that one—tilted cervix and very fertile woman right here! By the way, it doesn't cause any problems with child-birth either.*

A tilted cervix does, however, cause pain at times during intercourse. This can make any woman with this unusual cervix position want to avoid sex. This, of course, will hurt her chances at conception.

WHICH POSITION DO YOU STAND BY?

There are many old wives tales out there and other "facts" that can be misleading. Do you know which is which? Let's figure out if you hold the right position on each of these! Science has all the facts, so let's play a little Mommy Mythbuster, shall we?

1. **Whitey tighties could hinder men's fertility—** FICTION. Men *can* have fertility problems due to a condition where their testicles are excessively warm. Some people believe briefs, which can slightly warm a man's scrotum, can cause this decrease in sperm production similar to the way the condition does. It's simply just a myth.

2. **It'll take you longer the first go-around—**FICTION. About 60% of all cases of infertility happen to those women who have already had at least one baby. It's *much* more common to have challenges during a second or subsequent time of "trying to conceive" than it is the first go-around.

3. **If you watch a romantic movie, it'll up your chances at pregnancy—**FACT! Viewing a sexy movie, not X-rated, just romantic, with your spouse raises your progesterone level. Progesterone is a

hormone that prepares your uterus to house that newly fertilized egg.

4. **Having sex before bed is best**—FICTION. There really is no magical time that is best to have relations. Sure, some people will tell you that your husband's sperm count might actually be higher upon waking, but science says that if there is a difference, it's minute. *Who has time for that in the mornings anyway?! Although...*

5. **Stay laying down *after* sex with your legs in the air if you want to get pregnant**—FACTION (a mix of fact and fiction). This is one of those things they *might* have *half* right. Standing up directly after you finish having sex can discourage those little guys from getting to your cervix since gravity will pull them in the other direction. Staying on your back *does* give them an advantage. You see, your vaginal canal naturally slopes down, so your man's little guys are pooled that much closer to your egg, so it couldn't hurt to lay there for ten or fifteen minutes. However, there is no scientific evidence that it actually helps. *I guess if you're going to stay laying down after you have sex*

anyway, then before bed might be the best time for you after all!

Lying with your legs in the air? That may just give you very tired legs. Dr. Christopher Williams said that it most likely doesn't help much either. Dr. Williams is a reproductive endocrinologist and the author of "The Fastest Way to Get Pregnant Naturally."

6. **If you drink lots and lots of green tea, you will get pregnant**—FICTION. There's no evidence that green tea will aid in conception. Although there's a possibility that it *may* directly affect ovulation and fertility, experts don't know if green tea is all in a positive manner or not. It does contain folate, which is natural folic acid, making it good for pregnancy. It also contains a mineral, called polyphenols, which can help improve your blood flow and reduce inflammation. That's a great thing during pregnancy!

Sasha Watkins, a dietician, said a few cups of green tea won't hurt you, but it does have caffeine in it. She said that, although caffeine hasn't been linked to difficulty in conceiving, it can bring about health problems.

7. **You can choose whether to have a boy or girl by timing your sex just right**—FICTION. In the 1960s, Dr. Landrum Shettles developed the Shettles Method, which states that having relations closer to ovulation allows the males (Y) sperm, which travels the fastest, to get to the egg first. His method states that if you want to have a girl (X sperm), you should have sex three days before you ovulate instead. Your vaginal pH is acidic at that time and, therefore, the more fragile male (Y) sperm finds the environment more hostile. According to his theory, this gives the female (X) sperm the advantage.

Though it sounds reasonable and plausible, Dr. Shettles' theory has been found to be a myth. The *New England Journal of Medicine* conducted a study on the subject. They found absolutely no connection between the choosing of the baby's sex and when the couple has sexual relations. There have been people who've said, "His method worked for me." I'm sorry to burst your bubble, but luck is awesome!

8. **Sperm races quicker if it's well-lubed**—also FICTION. This *may* put a yellow light on conception, slowing the sperm to a crawl by 60-100% within sixty

183

minutes of intercourse. There are many formulas out there that have a pH balance that actually negatively affects those little men, making them sluggish. Standard, water-based lubes are some of them. If you find yourself absolutely needing lubrication, use hydroxyethyl cellulose-based lube. Also, some lubrication includes spermicide. You obviously don't want that! Read those labels carefully.

**Another quick note: Though oral sex is an excellent form of foreplay, using saliva for a lubricant is a bad idea when you're trying to conceive. Saliva isn't sperm-friendly at all. But, who's to say you can't have a little "foreplay" *after* Mr. Sperm has had his few minutes worth of time inside your canal to find his way northward a bit?

9. **Cough syrup will boost fertility**—FACT. Guaifenesin, the active ingredient in cough syrup, is shown, through research, to enhance fertility. In fact, some doctors prescribe guaifenesin to help thin out the cervical mucus of those women who have fertility problems due to thick mucus. Because it does help to thin the mucus, it'll help sperm to get through to the egg easier.

184

NOTE!!! MAKE SURE YOUR COUGH SYRUP DOESN'T HAVE ANY ANTIHISTAMINES OR COUGH SUPPRESSANTS, LIKE DEXTROMETHORPHAN, IN IT! Antihistamines will dry out the mucus, making it more difficult for the sperm to travel into your cervix.

If you do plan to try this little trick out, try using Guaifenesin Extended-Release 600 mg tablets, which is what's directed on the box. If you have an allergy, sensitivity, or aversion to Guaifenesin, you might try Mucinex Expectorant or two teaspoons of just plain old Robitussin expectorant (generic will work just fine) three times a day. You don't want there to be any extra letters (*including love letters*) attached to the end of the "Robitussin" name on the bottle. It's suggested you only take these during the seven days or so of your fertile window (we'll talk about this in the next chapter) so you don't get too much of the medicine. This bears repeating: MAKE SURE there are no cough suppressants, antihistamines, or other active ingredients like dextromethorphan in them! You don't want to undo what you are trying to do!

10. **Add cinnamon to honey to increase your fertility—** FACT! Dr. Jane L. Frederick, FACOG, a fertility expert for Orange County Fertility, said that, not only can a cinnamon and honey mix actually aid in the blood flow to the reproductive organs, but, she said,

185

"raw honey contains amino acids that are helpful for ovarian function and can be beneficial to the reproductive system." Furthermore, cinnamon supplements helped women in a study at Columbia University Medical Center with polycystic ovarian syndrome to get their periods regulated! Polycystic ovarian syndrome, affecting one out of every ten women, is the leading cause of infertility in women.

11. **Oysters will make you more fertile**—FACT. This is scientifically proven to be true. Not only does it make you "want more" of your partner, but it's full of zinc, one of the most fertile vitamins nature has in her stores.

12. **To have a baby quicker, eat more high-fat dairy**— FACTION. In 2007, a link was found between low ovulation-related infertility and a low-fat dairy diet. Ever since then, high-fat dairy has been hailed as a "miracle baby maker." The truth is, as we've seen in recent chapters, you just need to watch what you eat on all levels. Nutrition is what's important. Pamela Frank, a naturopathic doctor based in Toronto, said that "carbs and sugars can be detrimental to conception because they require higher levels of insulin, which

can disrupt hormone balance." She also said that if you just eat healthy, whole foods and avoid herbicides, pesticides, and chemicals that disrupt the hormones (like BPA), you'll be better off. These healthy whole foods might consist of lean proteins, organic fruits or vegetables, nuts and seeds, and legumes.

13. Don't fret, you'll probably be blessed with a boy if it takes you a while to get pregnant anyway— FACT. *First of all, what if you want a girl? No help there!* The longer it takes you to conceive, the thicker your cervical mucus is likely to be. Though scientists haven't figured out why yet, your boy (Y) sperm finds an advantage there. Some theorize that the boy sperm are lighter since they contain less DNA and can, therefore, swim more quickly through the thick mucus.

So many old wives' tales, myths, and facts so extravagant they seem like fiction have been told over the years concerning conception that it's sometimes hard to distinguish fact from fiction. I hope this little list will help you a little in your quest toward conception! Just out of curiosity, though, what positions did you take on these matters? Did you win my little game of Mommy

Mythbuster? Were you in the right, or were you positionally incorrect?

There is one thing to remember. I said this about the supplements, and I will repeat it here about fertility boosters. DO NOT try "fertility helps," especially the guaifenesin "secret," without first talking to your doctor about it. There are many other old wives' tales out there, too, that may seem reasonable (and may even be true) that require you to do something that could possibly be harmful. **Always** wait to consult with your doctor on them first.

You'll reach your perfect "when" when the time is right. It can become an unhealthy obsession to try to rush it too fast. If you're wanting to press it forward, though, and there's nothing wrong with that, there are some other things you can do—and I'm not talking about the scary, unhealthy, unpractical, and downright dangerous things some people have tried. After we get you on the right road, so you're not "positionally incorrect," we'll get you started on charting. Next chapter, everyone!

CHAPTER THREE: YOUR PERFECT

WHEN

Every good cook knows that timing is vital. Leave the broccoli in too long, it turns to mush. Don't cook the rice long enough, it's crunchy and sticks to your teeth. Take the bread out of the oven too soon, and it falls, leaving a sad, misshapen loaf—if you can call it that.

Timing is vital to pregnancy too! Yes, it's the classic "boy meet girl," as the sperm and the egg join, creating a new, little life, but there's only a **very** short window each month that it can happen in—a magic period, your "perfect when."

Do you know when you're the most fertile? Do you really know your body? When should you be "trying" in order to get pregnant more quickly? How do you know when that "perfect when" is? This is where charting your fertility really begins to play in.

****CHARTING YOUR FERTILITY****

You can have relations so often that your insides jiggle when you walk and still fail to get pregnant if you don't hit your "perfect when." Charting is one of the ways to make this happen. Being aware of your fertile days leads to a positive test in just about 90% of all instances, the American Pregnancy Association tells us.

Knowing when you ovulate is a big step toward being pregnant with your bundle of joy. Let me tell you why. Ovulating is when your ovaries drop an egg. The perfect time for your egg to get fertilized is when it is traveling down your fallopian tubes. Since your egg will only live for twelve to twenty-four hours and since your man's sperm will live close to five days, your perfect "when," or time to have sex, will be right before you ovulate or on the day of. The only way you can make a go at fertilizing that egg is to know beforehand when you will ovulate.

"BEFOREHAND??!!! WHAT?! HOW?!"

There are several ways to figure out when you are ovulating, but, whichever method or combination of methods you plan to use, the best way to learn your perfect "when" is to chart for a few months to get to know your body and its cycles.

THE HOW-TO OF CHARTING

<u>Step One</u>: On a calendar, mark the first day of your menstrual cycle. *Simple right?* Since your period will always be changing things up on you, do this for a few months.

<u>Step Two</u>: Average the lengths of several cycles (from the first day of each cycle to the day before the next) to give yourself the typical number of days your cycle lasts. Contrary to popular belief, your cycle is **not** *just* when you're menstruating. It lasts throughout the entire month, thus the term "monthly cycle."

<u>Step Three</u>: Take your shortest cycle and subtract eighteen days from the end it. Do the same with the longest, subtracting eleven days from its length. The seven days between are the days you're going to want to hit "it" fast and furious. These are the days you will most probably be the most fertile, making one of those days your perfect "when."

WHY CHART?

Why chart!? WHY chart!? Why, I ought to...! No, in all seriousness, though, there are several reasons to chart your cycle, figuring out your fertile days:

- Odds are that you don't have that perfect "twenty-eight-day cycle every single month" body. Healthy cycles can last anywhere from twenty-eight to thirty-six days. Several things can vary this number, changing it up even every month! It's hard to know when you're going to ovulate if you don't even know when your period's coming... or when it started to begin with.

Don't you hate those OB/GYN visits—"How long since your last period?" they ask. They *always* ask it, yet I'm always left there with a blank stare on my face as I try to calculate how many days it's been since my last. Usually, I figure it out based on certain "landmarks"—I was wearing a pad at church last Sunday, and I know I started a few days before then, but I wasn't flowing yet on Thursday because I wasn't worried about peeing in the cup at the Urologist's." More often than not, it's something like, "I really wanted to have sex on Wednesday, but we had to wait 'til after church because Matt had to work late. By the time church was over and we had gotten home, I had started my period. Therefore... I started on Wednesday of last week." By the way, ladies, that's a sign to watch for! Some women get horny near the beginning of a new cycle.

- Even if your body does happen to give you the good fortune of being the perfect "twenty-eight day every month-er," you may not ovulate every single cycle. When you do, though, which'll be most of the time (*hopefully, right?!*), that little egg will pop out anywhere between day twelve and day sixteen, with day one of your cycle being the first day of your period.

- It's essential to know the days you're fertile since your egg is only hospitable for twelve to twenty-four hours. After that, she just withers up and is reabsorbed back into your body. You need to have sperm either ready and waiting when your egg is dropped or at least on their way toward your egg when she's popped out of your ovary. Sperm can take eight or more hours to fight their way upstream (*Remember, they're minuscule creatures even you can't see. It's a LOOONG trek for them*)! Knowing when you're about to be fertile makes a big difference in your journey towards pregnancy since you can then have a better idea of when to start those little men on their journey of love.

- Another reason to chart is that it's a good way to find many medical problems, the most pertinent right now being the discovery of a short luteal phase—from the time you ovulate to the time you "start" once more. We'll call this phase "Post-Ovulation." This phase of the cycle can typically last anywhere between twelve and sixteen days. Through charting, you may find this phase to last a much shorter amount of time. If this is the case, it may be harder to become pregnant, or you may be more apt to miscarriages. Your endometrium (the lining on your uterus, which gives that baby a spot to implant really well) has less time to thicken. This can be corrected if it is known about. We'll talk more thoroughly about luteal defects later in this chapter.

BREAKING IT ALL DOWN

I find it interesting that a woman's psyche cycles through four phases a month (Reflective, Dynamic, Expressive, Creative). The moon cycles through four basic phases a month (New Moon, Waxing Moon, Full Moon, and Waning Moon). There are four seasons. There are four respiratory stages (Inspiration, End-Inspiration, Expiration, End-Expiration) and four stages of the sexual response cycle (excitement, plateau, orgasm, resolution). Even so, your "monthly cycle" includes four phases from the time of your "first bleed" to the last day of freedom every month. Your body's four phases are:

- Your Period

- Pre-Ovulation

- Ovulation

- Post-Ovulation (Luteal Phase)

Let's look at each of these more in depth.

PHASE ONE: Your Period

Day One—When your uterus sheds the endometrium on day one of your cycle, which is the lining that builds up in the uterus during the post-ovulation phase. It causes bleeding and discharge. This usually lasts an average of three to seven days but can last for a longer or shorter time depending on the person and the circumstances in their life. The length and timing of your period can be affected by several things, like strenuous exercise, stress, or health problems and more.

Day Three—By day three of your period, your estrogen and progesterone levels begin to rise. This causes your body to start the process or rebuilding your endometrium. The endometrium is very important to the pregnancy process since this is what your baby will implant in—or attach to.

Day Four or Five—The next day (or the following), your ovaries will begin to prepare themselves for the release of one egg—or possibly two or three in rare circumstances, which may result in twins or triplets. This process the ovaries use to ready themselves for dropping an egg is called ripening the follicles.

By the way, did you know your body has all the eggs it will ever have when you're born? Don't worry! Once you reach puberty (the average age is fifteen), you'll still have between 300,000 and 500,000 eggs and maybe more! Once you reach puberty, you'll begin losing up to 1,000 eggs a month (only the most mature will be released). Don't worry yourself too much, though. According to www.acog.org, you'll still have around 25,000 eggs when you reach 37-years-old. And, at age 51 (the average age women reach menopause), you'll still have about 1,000 eggs to go!

You don't have to concern yourself again with your ovaries at all in this phase. Your ovaries won't do anything else until around day fourteen when they actually drop the egg. That's a different phase altogether.

It's almost impossible to get pregnant on your period, so there's no reason to push yourself to have sex during this time if you don't feel like it. Cramps, a bloody mess, ill-temper, and whatever other individual symptoms you may experience along with your period, if any, may not be conducive to a desire for relations.

PHASE TWO: Pre-Ovulation

Dr. Kelly Pagidas, a fertility specialist who works on staff at the Woman and Infants Center for Reproduction and Infertility in Providence, recommends that those trying to conceive have sex every other day, if possible, starting right after the period phase has ended.

Around Day Seven—You know that nasty, inconvenient discharge that makes you wonder if you have a yeast infection every month? This starts around day seven. Your body will begin indicating fertility will come soon by excreting this vaginal discharge. You can track ovulation by your cervical mucus, so pay attention to what it looks and feels like. Your cervical mucus will seem a little springy to the touch on day seven. *Oh! Don't look at your book like that! Yes, I said, "what it feels like." Pick up your jaw. If you want to track your fertility using your fertility via cervical mucus (the cheapest way to do it), you'll have to look and it and touch it. It's not as gross as you think.*

You know how you always get that slippery gush that makes you think you started your period early and how it always seems to be in an "uh-oh moment" when there's absolutely nothing you can do about that right then? You know how that mucus, over a short amount of time, goes from clear to cloudy and thick to elastic feeling? You know that thick slime, like an egg yolk, just hanging there after every poop? Yeah… meet your pre-ovulation mucus, ladies! This is your cervical mucus. It's simply vaginal discharge. It comes along before ovulation. It aids the sperm and egg by making the "meet-up place" more habitable for fertilization. You're more fertile when your cervical mucus is like egg whites—clear, slightly stretchy, and slippery.

Around Day Nine to Day Eleven—Between day nine and eleven, it'll become creamy and white. Fertility is on its way. Your ovary hasn't released its egg yet—you see, usually, only one ovary releases an egg a month (unless, of course, your body plans multiple pregnancies), and there is no rhyme or reason as to which ovary will be chosen. However, your cervical mucus is sperm friendly around this time, even extending the sperm's life, giving it a five-day lifespan once it's trapped inside. It's a good idea to get some sex in then, even before ovulation, so you have some swimmers in there, ready to fertilize your egg as soon as it drops. Remember, I said earlier that an egg only lives twelve to twenty-four hours? If you have some little men in place before you ovulate, you have a better chance of one catching the egg during that short window of fertility. Doctors suggest having sex every other day during this fertile time.

PHASE THREE: Ovulation

Around Day Fourteen—Your egg will drop! Welcome to your "perfect when"! The problem, and the BIG reason for charting, is that many woman's ovulation phases differ greatly. On an average, many women's ovulation begin around fourteen days before their next period is scheduled to start, but when is that supposed to be? One way to figure that out is to chart your cycles, thus the reason for this chapter.

There are many different ways to forecast ovulation in order to get it charted on your calendar:

1. By paying attention to your symptoms:

- Your breasts will be tender or more tender than usual.

- Your cervical mucus will thin.

- To the joy of your partner, your sex drive will kick into high gear.

- The sensations you feel during sex will be increased. *Yay!!*

- The pain in one side of your lower abdomen may be dull or stabbing, depending on each woman, but this is a symptom of the egg pushing its way through your ovary.

- Your basal (base/ resting) body temperature will decrease by one degree when you're about to ovulate. It will increase by a half a degree to one degree when you're ovulating or have already ovulated, but by the time it does that, it may be too late to try to have sex and get those little sperm dudes up there to catch up with your eggs. Remember, it can take up to eight hours for the little guys to make it to the egg, which may only live, on the low end, a total of twelve hours. If your body drops that egg in the middle of the night, your egg may only have five or six hours until certain demise.

2. <u>By taking your basal body temperature</u>—"But," you might ask, "if my temperature only rises and falls by a fraction of a degree, how am I supposed to tell?" Easy! There's a special thermometer called a basal body thermometer. *Convenient, right?* It's a large thermometer that only reads from 96 to 100 degrees Fahrenheit and reads within one-tenth of a degree. This works out because most of us have a basal body temperature of 96 to 98 before we ovulate and of 97 to 99 after. This may be a quick or gradual change. The rise in temperature is caused by the increase of progesterone in the body.

You must make sure to take your basal body temperature every morning every single day at the same exact time. It must be taken as soon as you awake and before you eat, drink, talk, or even move. Be sure not to speak or move at all while you're taking your temperature either. This must be a complete resting body temperature!

Follow the directions exactly as they are listed on the packaging that come with your thermometer. First, you'll insert the thermometer into your vagina. Leave it there for at least five minutes. Read your basal body temperature within one-tenth of a degree and record your daily temperature on your fertility chart. Record your numbers for a few months until you have a running temperature for those months and have a good idea of which day you're ovulating on each month. This can be tricky since your body can switch it up from month to month. It should give you a window of when to "go for the gold."

Sometimes it can be challenging to get an accurate basal body temperature reading. Some of the things that can affect your reading might be:

- Illness

- Being under emotional distress

- Not sleeping well

- Exhaustion

- Sleeping under an electric blanket

- Smoking

- Drinking alcohol

If you think any of these things might be interfering with a temperature reading, note that on your fertility chart along with the temperature reading. This is another reason for charting a few months. It's best to use a couple methods of determining ovulation along with monitoring basal body temperature. You should also chart your symptoms and your changes in cervical mucus. You could possibly even add an ovulation predictor kit, which can be found in most drugstores.

3. By monitoring your cervical mucus—We've already spoken about this, so I won't spend too much time on it. Perform a quick test by grabbing a sample of cervical mucus out of your vagina with your finger and thumb. Tap them together. To signify your "perfect when," your mucus should be spread easily, being thin and slippery, the consistency of egg whites, and there should be more of it than there is typically.

4. By use of Ovulation Predictor Kits (OPKs)—Nowadays, doctors suggest using OPKs. They advise that they give a more accurate prediction of when you'll ovulate than any of the other three methods. With this method, you simply pee on a stick starting nine days after your period started and keep peeing on it until it gives you a positive result, as suggested by an associate professor of gynecology at Duke University Medical Center in Durham, N.C., Joanne

Piscitelli, MD. *And no, she's not talking about a limb off a tree, for those of you who are sarcastic in nature.*

Being able to detect a spike in the luteinizing hormone contained in your urine, OPKs give you advanced warning of your oncoming ovulation. In fact, this spike will provide you with a thirty-six to forty-eight-hour notice before ovulation.

5. <u>By the use of new technological advances</u>—Charting can seem intimidating. There's so much to keep up with even though it's not that hard if you just do it step by step. However, in a day and age where everyone utilizes the apps on their phones, tablets, and laptops to keep up with their world, fertility technology for tracking or testing for ovulation makes sense. My phone and computer are my calendar, memory, organizer, shopping list, bill reminder, and even my kids' schedule for their schoolwork (I homeschool). I'd be lost without them. Many people are the same. I will list seven great options for you and one bonus:

    - *Ovia Fertility*—This app lets you know what day a pregnancy test will first show results. *Pretty cool, right!* It tracks your cervical fluid, basal body temperature, cervical position, medications, and more. It also gives you cycle insights and daily tips on trying to conceive.

It does many other things, including offering an accurate ovulation predictor and letting you know the area surrounding your "perfect when." It provides a calendar for charting PMS, symptoms, sex, mood, and exercise and nutrition. The app syncs with wearables that are popular for fitness, like Jawbone, Fitbit, and Nokia. It provides access to over 2,000 articles on conception, fertility, and reproductive health written by experts, integrates with Apple Health, thereby offering you suggestions on how to take a more holistic view to your health; and, allows you to ask questions in a forum of other users. Not only that, but it's completely possible to export all your data into Excel. Ovia Fertility is a free app and is compatible with both iOS and Android.

- *Glow: Fertility and Ovulation Tracker for Pregnancy*— You simply enter your information, just like you would on a paper fertility chart (symptoms, mood, basal body temperature, menstrual cycle, ovulation, etc.), and, here's the plus, it will predict your "perfect when" days for you. This app is free for Android and iOS. However, there is a fee if you want to subscribe to use anything above their free service.

- *Clearblue Connected Ovulation Test System*—This ovulation test is actually Bluetooth enabled, able to hook directly to your smartphone! It will sync the data from each test to your phone through the Clearblue Connected app. This app will effortlessly tidy away your fertility information into its memory. *Yes, I just said that. Oh my goodness! I sounded like my grandma! I'm way too young for that!* This system will pick up on the surge in your luteinizing hormone that comes with your approaching ovulation, and with 99% accuracy, I might add. To top it all off, the app will send you reminders when it's time to test! *How great is that!* Clearblue Connected Ovulation Test System starts at $45.

- *Kindara Fertility and Ovulation*—Do you want to know more about basal body temperature and cervical changes when trying to conceive while tracking fertility and ovulation? Try Kindara! This app is free and works with iOS and Android. It's also possible to purchase an oral thermometer that works along with it. Though you don't **have** to have it, it does increase the accuracy of the results, automatically syncing to the Kindara app and helping you determine your "perfect when." This thermometer is called *Wink* and runs around $129.

- *Tempdrop*—This is a wearable, kind of like a step tracker, but this is a fertility tracker instead. You wear it on your upper arm at night. While you sleep, it gathers all kinds of information, using multiple sensors and thousands of data points, surrounding your basal body temperature and movement. Tempdrop syncs with whichever pregnancy app you choose to log your information with, as it can be synced with several different ones, offering a varied choice. This device runs right at $150.

- *EarlySense Percept Ovulation and Fertility Sensor*—If you really detest peeing on your fingers while trying to pee on a stick, and who doesn't, and if a wearable doesn't really fit your fancy, there's always the EarlySense Percept. It's a highly sensitive sensor that goes under your mattress. It uses sound waves to pick up on your heart rate and breathing. The device sends the data it collects right to your smartphone, which stores it in the Percept app. The sensor is $199, but the app is free.

- *Ava Bracelet*—Another wearable, this one is a bracelet instead and is, obviously, worn on your wrist. This gadget is also worn during sleep. Ava measures your skin temperature, resting pulse rate, heat loss, sleep, and five other parameters. Come morning, you merely sync the bracelet to the app on your phone, which then tells you if you're fertile or not. Ava makes the claim that the bracelet averages an 89% accuracy at detecting approximately 5.3 fertile days every cycle. That would be an average of 4.3 days before ovulation and the day of. The app is free, the bracelet will sync with iOS and Android, The Ava Bracelet, however, is $249.

- BONUS—Another app that might help during your fertility journey is *Expectful*. Stress can affect fertility. *Expectful* offers guided meditations based on which stage of your journey you happen to be in, whether you're trying to conceive, newly pregnant, or in a later trimester. They even have meditations for new moms! This app is compatible with any device and runs $9.99/ month after a free trial.

Has trying to conceive become boring? A chore? A duty? It doesn't have to be! Make it fun. Switch it up. Just make sure that you and your partner are both comfortable with whatever "fun" thing you choose to go with. Here are some fun ideas to help get yourself and your partner in the mood:

- Play Strip Poker.

- Go commando.

- Make up a good sex story together.

- Role-play. Maybe act out your story or pretend to be masseuse and client getting a *full* body massage. There are so many options. Use your imagination!

- Take a hot shower together. One of you soap up and then use your body to soap up the other person. Lotion each other up afterward, taking your time and enjoying that skin on skin contact.

There are so many ideas out there. Choose one and go with it.

PHASE FOUR: Post-Ovulation

Approximately Day Fifteen thru Day Twenty-Eight or Later—This phase goes by a second name as well, the luteal phase. The last phase of your cycle, post-ovulation can last anywhere from twelve to sixteen days. In this phase, your progesterone rises. Progesterone is the hormone that causes the endometrium, or uterus lining, to thicken and also tells your ovaries to stop dropping eggs, preventing miscarriage. According to the Association of Women for the Advancement of Research and Education, if your progesterone isn't high enough and your ovaries do drop an egg, your uterus will automatically shed the endometrium, thinking it's "period time," and the developing baby along with it.

In this phase, the thin and sperm-friendly cervical mucus will dry up completely, creating a plug in your cervix. This plug will keep any more sperm from getting into your uterus. There's no need for them to be there. *Sorry, little guys, you're too late... No admittance.*

Around Day Twenty—Six days after your egg is fertilized, it will implant (hopefully) in your endometrium. Your human chorionic gonadotropin (hCG) will begin to rise. Human chorionic gonadotropin is the hormone that will register your pregnancy on the home pregnancy test within the next week or two depending on the test you use.

Trouble Post-Ovulation

If you have more frequent periods, trouble getting pregnant, miscarriage, or spotting between periods, you may possibly have a luteal phase defect. These defects can cause the endometrium to fail to respond to the progesterone, or your ovaries do not make enough progesterone at all.

You may ask, "What causes your ovaries to fail to make enough progesterone?" There are several reasons that I can think of, some of which we have already spoken about, but I will give you three of the main causes:

1. Xenoestrogens (Environmental Estrogens)—These things try to choke us out almost every moment of every day. They will make your body think you're suffering from estrogen dominance, which is where the estrogen in your body is higher than the progesterone in your body. Estrogen dominance causes a hormonal imbalance in your body that causes your ovaries to fail to produce enough

progesterone. Xenoestrogens can be found in our foods, plastics, synthetic hormones, animal products, and more.

2. Chronic Stress—*Lordy, Lordy! I'm ALL stress 24/7!* Cortisol, which our adrenal glands produce too much of when we're stressed, trying to soothe us, is another progesterone killer. Cortisol production, a protection response, kicks to the forefront before any other hormone production. This includes progesterone. Besides that, it also jams the signals between the progesterone and its receptors.

It's not a wonder that stress makes it harder to get pregnant. If it lowers the progesterone in such a way, it's a wonder any of us can have kids! In this fast-paced world, everyone seems to be so stressed, and I bet you fall into that category too.

Make sure you take some time for yourself each day. Read a book for a few minutes before bed, take a hot bath before crawling between the sheets, or get a well-deserved massage from your one and only. Take a trip to the mall, do a hobby, get your nails done, go on a date with hubby, whatever, just do something for you. Relax. Destress.

3. Excessive Exercise—"But... Isn't exercise good for you?" Yes, but too much of anything, even a good thing, can be bad. Not only can excessive exercise affect you

emotionally, but it can have an adverse effect on you physically as well, specifically in the area of hormones. It wreaks havoc on your progesterone levels in particular.

The luteal phase defect can be caused by several health problems as well. A few include:

- Endometriosis

- Anorexia

- Hyperprolactinemia

- Exercising in extreme amounts

- Polycystic ovary syndrome

- Obesity

- Thyroid disorders

Often, if these health conditions or other conditions are treated, the luteal phase defect can be corrected, and you can go on to have a healthy pregnancy.

A doctor can diagnose a luteal phase defect, but it can be complicated as no one test can be used to diagnose it. Some tests that might be run during the search for answers may include blood tests that measure your luteinizing hormone level, follicle-stimulating hormone level, or progesterone levels or a pelvic ultrasound to evaluate how thick your endometrium gets.

If you are diagnosed with a luteal phase defect, your treatment will depend on your overall health. For those who are not trying to conceive, no treatment is necessary. That does not apply to you. In your case, of course, any conditions that can lead to a luteal phase defect must be corrected first. Next, if correcting the condition does not fix the defect, there are some medications that your doctor might suggest:

- **Clomiphene citrate (Clomid).** This medication will trigger your ovaries to create more follicles. Follicles, if you remember, are the part of the ovaries that release eggs. Follicles are the part of the ovaries that produce the progesterone. With more follicles, your progesterone levels will rise.

- **Human chorionic gonadotropin (hCG).** This may jumpstart <u>ovulation</u>, causing them to produce more progesterone.

- **Progesterone injections, suppositories, or pills.** These medications can be used after you have ovulated. This added progesterone will assist the endometrium in its growth.

Can We Do This Without Medication?

Nutrition is always the best place to start in any circumstance. The foundation for anything "health," hormonal health included, is diet. Are you getting enough of the vitamins and minerals you need through the foods you eat to cure your progesterone deficiencies? If not, why? If it's not possible for you to get all the vitamins you need, supplement. There are also botanicals you'll want to consider.

YOUR DIET:

- Lower your physical symptoms that are created from your low progesterone and PMS by getting at least two to four cups of leafy, green veggies in every day. Some examples might be collard greens, mustard greens, swiss chard, kale, and spinach. These foods are high in B-complex vitamins, which are essential vitamins for regulating your hormones. It doesn't matter if they're raw or cooked but cooking them tends to cook some of the vitamins out, so please be careful not to cook much of your greens or to cook them for too long.

- You can actually increase your progesterone levels by getting at least 75mg of vitamin C a day. However, you should really aim for 750mg daily if you want the maximum benefit this has to offer. Brussel sprouts, bell peppers, oranges, papaya, and strawberries are some of the foods that are high in vitamin C. For a more complete list, refer to PART ONE: Chapter Five.

- I know this goes against everything you've heard, but you want to make sure to get plenty of dietary cholesterol. *Eat the things with the good cholesterol in them, silly, not the bad, and you'll be fine.* You want foods like pastured eggs,

216

organic grass-fed animal protein, and grass-fed butter. Healthy, but definitely not cholesterol-free. Progesterone is synthesized from a hormone, called pregnenolone, which hails from none other than cholesterol itself.

- Halibut, chia seeds, wild-caught salmon, walnuts, and sardines are all excellent sources of a particular essential fatty acid, called omega-3. These will help to bring up your progesterone level as well. Make sure to get lots of omega-3 in your diet.

SUPPLEMENTS AND BOTANICALS:

- Taking vitamin B6 will make an extreme difference in your hormonal health. This B vitamin was found to be much more effective in the post-ovulation phase than any other B vitamin it ran up against. You should take a 50mg B6 and a B-Complex as well. The B vitamins all work together, all of them giving each other a leg up. You shouldn't get more than 100mg of B6 daily. An overdose can cause nerve toxicity.

- A daily regimen of 15mg of the spice, saffron, which you can purchase in a capsule, can treat a few of the symptoms of low progesterone. These include painful periods, depression, and PMS.

- Proven in studies to raise progesterone, Chasteberry, at 1,000mg daily, makes the body produce more of the luteinizing hormone. This hormone prompts the ovaries to drop an egg. The follicle, then, does its job, thus increasing the production of progesterone.

Once we've learned to chart, it's time to move on to learning how to increase fertility. As stated earlier, charting helps move things along up to 90% of the time, but it can take up to a year to get pregnant! If you know what kinds of things to do to increase fertility, you can increase your chances at a swift and healthy conception that much quicker. We'll cover this in Chapter Four.

CHAPTER FOUR: INCREASING FERTILITY

Charting is a great way to discover your fertile times, but what if your fertile times aren't fertile enough? I was very fertile. Once my husband and I went off the patch, we were pregnant within three months, and we weren't trying! In fact, we were using the withdrawal method *and* the calendar method to avoid pregnancy! We had gone off the patch for religious reasons. We had not used condoms due to an allergy, and the price of the skins was expensive—*if they were even a thing back then (??).* We did have a miscarriage the first time around, but then we were pregnant again before I even had my next cycle! Sierra stuck tight. She's twelve-years-old now and a full-out teen attitude in a pre-teen body... *Oh boy!!!* She's the first of four children (six pregnancies total).

Sometimes, even when you're filling those sheets regularly, though, trying your best to get that baby bump started, fertilization can seem mysterious, just out of arms reach. You may not be able to do anything about some of the things that affect fertility, like your age, but there are other things you have control over. Let's explore them!

Diet

A problem that affects up to 15% of women, infertility can be improved by up to 69% by a simple lifestyle and diet change. "Really?!" you say. *Yup. Really.* For instance, you can increase fertility by simply eating foods that are rich in certain vitamins and in antioxidants.

Antioxidants

Antioxidants disable those free radicals that can damage the egg cells in your body and the sperm cells in your spouse's. Also, according to NCBI, there was a study done in which the men who ate just 75 grams of walnuts daily, which are rich in antioxidants, was found to have improved sperm motility, vitality, and morphology! A second study of 60 couples eating foods full of antioxidants showed a 23% greater rate of conception in those undergoing in-vitro fertilization.

Vegetables, fruits, berries, grains, and nuts are stuffed full of vitamins and antioxidants that are advantageous to your body in your quest toward conception. They have vitamin C and E, lutein, and beta-carotene. According to NCBI, there were several studies conducted in which it was determined that spinach, asparagus, and berries had the highest antioxidant capacities. Extra virgin olive oil came in a close second.

VITAMINS IN YOUR DIET

- **B Vitamins**—Found in whole grains, meat, chickpeas, eggs, and leafy greens, all B vitamins help your ovaries release their egg come ovulation time. B6 will raise your progesterone level, which, as you know, is the hormone that maintains pregnancy.

- **Beta-carotene**—This helps in preventing early miscarriage by regulating your hormones once that baby burrows his way into his new home. Eat lots of butternut squash, carrots, kale, sweet potatoes, cantaloupe, spinach, and broccoli, as they are full of this essential phytonutrient.

- **Bromelain**—This is a group of enzymes. It's thought to help your fertilized egg to implant in your uterus. It can *only* be found in pineapples!

- **Vitamin C**—As you already know, this vitamin boosts immunity. What you probably didn't know is that it aids in the production of progesterone. If you have a luteal phase defect, it appears that vitamin C in strawberries, citrus, cherries, tomatoes, peas, and potatoes will promote your fertility. It will also help to improve your man's sperm motility and sperm health.

- **Coenzyme Q10 (CoQ10)**—This is a natural enzyme thought to improve egg and sperm quality dramatically. It's still in the animal testing phase, but it doesn't hurt to try! Scientists also hope it will help to reverse some of the signs of reproductive decline that is related to aging. It can be found as a supplement, or, as a better source, in organ meats (such as kidneys and heart meats), fish, and wheat germ.

- **Vitamin D**—Usually having a lower level of vitamin D, infertile women need to be sure to get plenty of this vitamin, which is vital for the production of sex hormones. Not only will it make you more fertile, but, there's a possibility that it may possibly help improve ovulatory dysfunction. You see, according to Yale University School of Medicine, of the many women with ovulatory dysfunction, 40% of them are clinically deficient of vitamin D.

Getting as little as 10 to 15 minutes of sunlight daily can improve your levels. It can also be found in fatty fish (such as tuna and salmon) and fortified dairy products.

- **Vitamin E**—Having potent antioxidant powers, this vitamin is surrounding your developing eggs. In rats, vitamin E deficiencies may be the cause of fertility problems. It has also been found that this vitamin has a direct effect on sperm health. Avocados, whole grains, almonds and other such nuts, sweet potatoes, seeds, and leafy greens, are some good sources of vitamin E.

- **Folic Acid**—You already know about this one, so this is just a basic reminder: Folic acid is a B vitamin—B9. As you know, you should take at least 400-600 mcg every day. I'll bet you didn't know, though, that those who faithfully take folate have less infertility that's ovulation-related! It's also great for your partner to take folate! It will help the sperm he produces to be healthier. In fact, according to the University of California Berkley, compared to men who don't have much folic acid in their bodies, guys with a higher level of folic acid reduces the number of abnormal sperm by 20%. One way you and your guy might get a higher folic acid content is by eating leafy greens, beans, fortified cereals and drinking orange juice.

- **Iron**—Yes, I know we already learned about iron too, but what we *didn't* learn is that if you get enough iron or even a little more than you need, you'll most likely not have all the ovulatory issues that you could have had otherwise. More iron through an additional supplement equals a 40% less chance of infertility according to statistics! Your doctor, of course, should be consulted before you add an extra supplement to your routine. You should not rely on supplements alone, as you already know. Be sure to add those eggs, beans, meats, beets, spinach, whole-grain cereals, tomatoes, broccoli, beets, spinach, and pumpkin! Non-heme iron foods are especially important, as is getting plenty of vitamin C to increase your body's ability to absorb this hard to absorb mineral.

- **Omega-3 fatty acids**—These are nutrients we cannot naturally produce but must be gotten from outside sources like mackerel, eggs from chickens fed omega-3s, cod, salmon, anchovies, sardines, walnuts, and herring. They'll increase the blood flow to your organs, like the uterus, aid in the release of your eggs, and help your body by balancing out your hormones.

- **Selenium**—A powerful detoxifier found in leafy greens, brazil nuts, fish, and whole grains, selenium is great for aiding estrogen metabolism and possibly aiding in defense of your egg against free radicals. These free radicals make your eggs to decline. It will also aid in the motility of your partner's sperm.

- **Zinc**—Be sure to get plenty of fish, oysters, eggs, meat, wheat germ, poultry, and pumpkin seeds, because low levels of zinc, according to the centers for the disease control and prevention, has been linked to early miscarriage. It will also improve the motility of your man's little guys and boost their general quality.

SUPPLEMENTS

Of course, any of the above can be taken as supplements, but they won't do you as much good. In fact, vitamins in tablet or pill form don't absorb as well into your body as natural vitamins do. Minerals and vitamins in supplements are artificial, of course, and not the real thing.

Scientifically speaking, according to a professor of nutrition at Georgia State University, Christine Rosenbloom, because they're "synthetic" doesn't mean they're inferior. Although the absorption of nutrients is not "well-studied," studies do seem to indicate that they absorb just as well as the natural forms of the vitamins and minerals do (other than vitamin E, which is absorbed much better in its natural form)... *if* the supplements disintegrate in your stomach.

DISSOLVING POWERS

The only problem with this "scientific evidence" is that many vitamins are found every day in septic tanks around the world... undissolved... undisintegrated... In fact, I have tried dissolving a certain prenatal vitamin and a couple different other vitamins in water to find them still almost fully intact the next day! You see, for the vitamin or mineral to absorb into your body, it **must** dissolve quickly. In fact, they must disintegrate within twenty-minutes to do the body any good. In a study, of forty-nine multivitamins studied, 51% didn't disintegrate at all. Supplements with a USP symbol are more likely to dissolve than other vitamins and minerals.

"So why don't multivitamins disintegrate?" *Good question!* First, that waxy, shiny, overcoat on them is actually made up of wax, shellac, and hydroxypropyl methylcellulose. The good thing about these coatings is that they keep the moisture out. The bad thing? It makes it harder to disintegrate since it works hard at... keeping all those fluids out.

Secondly, so many supplements these days are full of fillers, excipients, flow agents, and binders to make them *just* the right size or to help them bind together. These ingredients cause the capsules and tablets to have a hard time breaking down.

ABSORPTION

Let's talk absorption but just for a minute. The corn syrup and sugar added to some supplements may make them more appetizing, but they keep your body from absorbing micronutrients into your body. The sugar content is higher in gummy, chewable, and liquid vitamins. These sweeteners, which are usually genetically modified, will cause you to gain weight and also cause your insulin to spike.

So What's the Fix?

1. **Use a powder**—Using something that's already disintegrated for you, according to the American Pharmaceutical Association textbook, is "the most bioavailable [absorbable] form." There are a few micronutrients that can break down other micronutrients, too, in the liquid form, so the powder form is better.

2. **Pay close attention to the ingredients**—Say no to corn syrup, sugar, binders, fillers, artificial colors, excipients, and preservatives (BHA/ BHT).

3. **Study the competition**—Study them out. Which ones are the best? Which have the wax? Which absorb the best? Which are USP labeled? Which will best disintegrate within the necessary twenty minutes? Which will absorb into your system?

Vitamins as a Supplement

- Multivitamin— Yes, diet is the most important part found in increasing fertility, but, if you're not getting what you need through diet, a multivitamin, may also increase your level of fertility. To give yourself a 20% chance of missing ovulatory infertility, according to a study found on NCBI, simply take at least three multivitamins weekly. This is true even if you fail to get enough or all the minerals and vitamins listed above. A second study confirmed a 41% lesser infertility risk in those women taking multivitamins—especially multis that contain folate.

NATURAL SUPPLEMENTS

Vitamins and minerals are not the only supplements that increase fertility. There are natural supplements that are linked to an increase in fertility as well. However, most of the research in this area is still in the animal-based research stage, and much more research is required before scientists will know enough to know for sure if these supplements are beneficial to fertility or not. Until then, there's no harm in trying! A few of these supplements include:

- **Bee Pollen**—Even as pollen tickles our noses and makes us sneeze, it seems to be "good" at something else too!

Bee pollen improves fertility, and (*bonus!*) improves immunity and nutrition.

There are a few cases where nutrition is a cause of a woman's difficulties in conception. This bee product contains every nutrient out there that God has created to sustain health and, in essence, restore poor health. In fact, it's rich in every single mineral and vitamin out there and is so high in protein that it exceeds beef by more than 50%! With any improvement in health, if the infertility is nutrition-related, a healthy pregnancy comes closer to becoming possible.

On top of that, bee pollen raises your natural levels of estrogen production. Increased estrogen often allows the healthier eggs to be released during ovulation, and, of course, healthy eggs equals a better chance at a healthier pregnancy.

A study conducted on buck rabbits, according to NCBI, found that bee pollen improved their fertility and overall sperm quality. It also has the same effect on men. This increase in your man's sperm count will increase your chances of conception as well.

- **Bee Propolis**—An anti-inflammatory and immunity booster, it's been known for a bit for helping women with endometriosis. Now, studies reveal that it can help them even more! A preliminary study in *Fertility and Sterility*

(2003;80: S32) saw women who'd been unsuccessful at pregnancy for two years or more have a 40% more chance at conception after just nine months of taking bee propolis.

- **Maca**—A superfood that can be obtained through the food itself (picked fresh in Peru) or as a powder, capsule, or a tincture that can be taken daily, Maca increases progesterone. It helps to improve egg and sperm health and helps to balance hormones. Another great thing it does is fix up the endocrine system. If your endocrine system is out of whack, it can make it hard for you to get pregnant.

- **Royal Jelly**—Yet another byproduct, royal jelly, is the food made for the queen ant that helps her to lay her daily 2,000 eggs. It will also help to raise your fertility. If taken regularly, it will also improve the quality of your egg and its health. Royal jelly provides several vitamins including A, B, C, D, and E. It also provides the minerals, calcium and iron, sugars, amino acids, lipids, and fatty acids.

231

BELIEVE IT OR NOT!!

- **Starting the day right may improve your fertility!** A substantial breakfast may balance your hormones and increase ovulation by 30%, especially in the case of polycystic ovary syndrome, which is one of the most significant causes of infertility among women today. However, be sure that if you increase your calorie intake on your breakfast that you decrease the calories in your dinner. Otherwise, you're sure to pack on the pounds!

- **Low-carb it!** Not necessarily a "low-carb" diet, but a "low*er* -carb" diet, will regulate your menstrual cycle, lower your risk of ovulatory infertility by 78%, and reduce testosterone and insulin levels. Raised levels can cause, or at least contribute to, infertility. You see, highly processed carbs elevate insulin levels, which will cause your blood sugar to rise. This makes your pancreas kick into high gear, releasing insulin. Insulin levels that are too high may keep you from ovulating.

You want to eat more complex carbs (fruits, beans, fiber, whole grains, etc.) instead of the simple carbs that spike your sugar. The "bad carbs" include things like white bread, cookies, white rice, and cakes. "Good carbs" gradually affect your insulin levels.

Grains that are just barely refined are chock-full of B vitamins, which, as we know, are fertility-friendly! Buckwheat, a great complex carb for you to eat, actually improves ovulation!

- **Trans fats bring with them a risk of infertility.** Healthy fats actually boost fertility. A few of these might be grass-fed beef, coconut, avocado, extra virgin olive oil, dark chocolate (*yum!*), nuts and nut butter, and whole eggs. Eat these healthy fats instead of trans fats.

Baked goods, processed foods, fried foods, some kinds of margarine, and many hydrogenated vegetable oils are full of trans fats. The reason these fats are linked to ovulatory infertility is that they impair insulin sensitivity. This leads to high blood sugar, which, again, impedes ovulation. Eating trans fats may actually raise your chances of ovulatory-related infertility by a whopping 31%. Trading out your carbs for trans fats raises it by an even higher risk—73%.

- **Eating more of your protein from vegetable sources is better.** The more meat protein you eat, the higher your chances are for ovulatory infertility. It raises those chances by 32%! You can lower your risks of ovulatory infertility by more than 50% by simply replacing just 5% of your total calories with vegetable protein (such as beans, nuts, and lentils) rather than protein from meat sources.

- **Eating more fiber can lead to a lower risk of ovulatory infertility.** According to one study, if you're over 32-years-old, simply increasing your daily intake of cereal fiber by 10 grams can lower your risk of ovulatory infertility by 44%! *However*, getting too much fiber may affect with your normal ovulation cycle, causing it to be "off."

Another good thing about fiber is that it will rid your body of excess estrogen. It will bind the estrogen to the fiber in the intestines and remove it with the other waste products. Some high-fiber foods include fruits, beans, whole grains, and vegetables.

- **Although low-fat dairy has been pushed on us, it may actually lower your chances of pregnancy.** If you replace just one serving (or more) of low-fat dairy with a high-fat dairy source daily (a glass of whole fat milk or a serving of full-fat yogurt, for instance), you can lower your chances of infertility by 27%. The Harvard School of Public Health's professor of epidemiology and nutrition and an author of the study surrounding this information, Walter Willet, M.D., confirms this.

Just as a note: Using Greek-style or homemade yogurt is best. These are some of the top fertility foods there are.

- **Alcohol isn't the only "drink" that affects fertility!** Yes, you should limit or even avoid drinking alcohol while trying to get pregnant since alcohol can cause problems in early pregnancy, but did you know that it can cause fertility problems too? It may change your estrogen levels and affect your baby's ability to implant.

Did you know alcohol isn't the only beverage that causes fertility problems? Caffeine also makes it hard to get pregnant. It takes an average of up to nine and a half months longer for you to conceive since it affects your hormone levels as well. You should stick with two cups or less of coffee a day. You shouldn't exceed 200 mg total of caffeine daily between any kind of caffeinated beverage you might drink—coffee, tea, and energy drinks, etc.

Another problem with caffeine is that it causes dehydration. Alcohol and caffeine both will cause your body to expel its fluids. As such, these drinks may cause your cervical fluid to change consistency, the mucus drying up a little due to the dehydration.

There are a few studies that show herbal tea may not do the same thing as orange pekoe or black tea do. In fact, these studies indicate that herbal teas may actually positively affect fertility!

As a note: Drinking a lot of caffeinated beverages before pregnancy may also cause miscarriage.

- **Exercise has more benefits than you realized!** We all know how good it is for our health, but did you know it's good for baby-making too? Yeah! It increases fertility! According to the Nurses' Health Study II, every hour spent exercising per week lowers your risk of infertility by a whopping 5%! As a matter of fact, lack of exercise brings with it the possibility of infertility.

On the other hand, too much exercise is bad in that excessive exercise can reduce your fertility. One study showed a 3.2 times greater risk of infertility among those whose daily routine included intensive exercise compared to those who didn't exercise at all. Here are some "rules" surrounding exercise while you're stuffing those sheets:

- o Firstly, quit putting off starting your exercise routine! Start now!

- o Find a routine that works for you now, so you'll be more likely to stick to it after conception.

- o Stick with your exercise routine, making it a habit, so it'll be easier to maintain.

o Have a list of things you can do to change up your routine. If you're in the habit of mixing up your exercise routine (varying what you do on different days), it'll help you stick to exercising—especially on days you have supposedly "valid excuses," like when it's pouring rain or when it's just "way too hot."

o One of the "mix it up" routines you should be doing is cardio, and that only at moderate-intensity. A few examples of moderate-intensity cardio might be swimming, power walking, or jogging. This will get your heartrate up regularly and help you build your endurance, which will also help you in delivery. Moderate-intensity exercise will also help you get into better shape while you're trying to conceive.

o Another is to strengthen your core muscles. Not only will this help you in building your list of the several different ways of doing your exercising, but it will also help tremendously with your pregnancy. You see, pregnancy makes your back hurt due to carrying all that extra weight out front. If your core is strong, it helps your back pain to lessen significantly by improving your posture and balance during the later months.

- o Getting to a healthy weight and staying there will improve your chances at conceiving more quickly, and exercise will help you get there, so get out there, get to work, and stay faithful!

- o Yes, exercise helps you lose weight, but don't focus on that. Don't get onto some fad diet to go along with your exercise routine. Don't forget, a balanced diet is also essential to fertility.

- o Remember! Stay away from that constant high-intensity training! That's a sure way to damage with your chances at conception. I'm sure you know people who've exercised all out and gotten pregnant just fine, but that doesn't mean it'll work for you. In fact, they should feel lucky that luck was on their side.

- **Unfermented soy may negatively affect fertility.** Soy in its most natural form is very healthy, but phytoestrogens, which are found in unfermented soy can cause fertility problems by interfering with hormone levels. You should avoid soy energy bars and powders, especially. These are

238

unfermented soy as well. Phytoestrogens mimic estrogen and disrupt the hormonal balance in the body. Your man, additionally, should keep from eating unfermented soy, as it may mess with his testosterone levels. Fermented soy, however, and whole soy are fine when they're consumed in moderation.

- **Eating *organic* fruits and vegetables may increase fertility.** "What?! What do you mean by that?" *Glad you asked!* The herbicides and pesticides used to kill the weeds and bugs on our vegetables and fruits are still there when they're served to us in the store. *Tasty, right?* They're believed to disrupt your period and hinder ovulation. They *will* for sure hurt your partner's fertility, however, causing lower-quality sperm and lowering his sperm count. If you're looking to conceive (and you are), avoid chemical-laden fruits and vegetable, reach for the organic ones, and make sure your partner does the same!

- **The toxins in cigarettes cause infertility.** Not only do they damage your eggs, which makes it hard for your egg to be fertilized and to implant in your uterus, but smoking causes your ovaries to age by several years. Due to this, if you're a smoker, your ovaries are less fertile than those of a non-smoker the same age as you are. The good news is that you do get some of that ovarian function back when you quit smoking, according to Robert Barbieri, M.D., the co-author of "6 Steps to Increased Fertility." Barbieri is also the head of obstetrics and gynecology at Brigham and Woman's Hospital, in Boston. He also tells us the bad news. That damage is permanent, so you never regain all your function back.

- **Industrial chemicals affect fertility.** I think this probably goes without saying. If you work a job with a hazardous chemical, always wear protective gear. Sometimes this gear isn't required, and it may not necessarily be essential for you either. You can check with the Center for Disease Control (CDC) to know for certain. Chemicals like nitrous oxide, radiation, jet fuel, and other certain common chemicals used in the industrial workplace can decrease fertility by disrupting your menstrual cycle.

- **Working a rotating shift causes 80% more fertility problems!** Even if you work a night shift, you'll have better success at conceiving than if you work a rotating schedule! If you think it may be at all possible, ask your boss for a steady shift. It may just help you hit the jackpot in baby land.

- **Douching can cause bacterial vaginosis, which can, subsequently, cause infertility, miscarriage, and preterm labor.** Douching takes out that normal bacteria that protects your vagina, giving way to the bad bacteria. *Oooooh. Sounds like the start of a bad horror movie.* This harmful bacteria gives way to bacterial vaginosis. Because grayish discharge and a fishy odor are the only signs, this common infection regularly goes unnoticed. And, of course, you know the rest of the story.

COMMON MISTAKES

We all get worried… sometimes for no reason at all. Sometimes we fail to worry when we should be worrying. I want to talk to you about one subject that we shouldn't worry about and two that many should and don't. These are three mistakes that are made all too often.

1. Don't be in a rush to see a specialist.

I know how easy it is to get frustrated when you're looking at pregnancy test after pregnancy test and seeing only one line every month, but, honestly, some people are calling the fertility specialist within three months of beginning their journey toward conception. It takes the average person six to twelve months to conceive. Of every couple out there that's trying to get pregnant, and this includes those who are older than 35 and those considered infertile:

- o Only 30% conceive after one month.

- o It takes 59% of women three months to conceive.

- o 80% won't conceive for up to six months.

- o And, 85% can take up to twelve months to get pregnant.

Specialists don't even want to see a healthy person until they've been trying for a year. Give it time!

**By the way,* while we're on the subject, let's talk about that word, "trying." You aren't "trying" if you're having sex only twice a month. You're not even "trying" if you're having sex four times a month the three days before your period starts. "Trying" is having intercourse at least every other day for at least the five days before ovulation and the day of ovulation. A gynecologic surgeon and assistant professor in the Department of Obstetrics and Gynecology at Northwest University Feinberg School of Medicine in Chicago, Angela Chaudhari, M.D., confirms this. There are some doctors out there that recommend that couples have relations a few times a week from day seven to day twenty in their cycle.

Note: You can look back at the last chapter, chapter three, for information on charting your cycle and, thus, having an idea of when you'll ovulate.

2. Don't fail to get help quickly enough.

There are some cases when rushing off to see the fertility doctor is not "rushing off" to see the fertility doctor at all. Sometimes, you should seek out a specialist before you even get pregnant. At other times, you'll need one within three months if you've not conceived and, at others, after six months. Below is the timeline the specialists would like for you to follow.

*You should see a specialist **before** "trying" if:*

o You've had several miscarriages or ectopic pregnancy;

o You have or have had a sexually transmitted infection;

- You've smoked in the past or smoke presently;

- Your periods are irregular and it has been at least three months since you've gotten off a hormonal birth control;

- You have polycystic ovarian syndrome (PCOS), endometriosis, or some other disorder such as these;

- You take long-term medication for a medical condition, such as epilepsy, diabetes, or severe depression, have a clotting or bleeding disorder, or have an autoimmune disease, like lupus;

- Or, your partner has fertility problems.

*See a fertility specialist **after three months** of trying if:*

- You're over 40-years-old.

*You should see a fertility specialist after "trying" **for six months** if:*

- You're between 35 and 40-years-old.

If you've overspent your amount of time and still haven't seen a specialist, call up your ob-gyn! A blood workup can be done.

Hormonal issues can be searched for. He can refer you to a reproductive endocrinologist if he or she sees it's needed.

If you're all good, your partner can get his sperm looked at by a urologist. He can get his health looked at. Lifestyle changes can be made, which can address many problems, by the way.

Even if it *is* infertility, there are so many assisted reproductive technologies out there. There's intrauterine insemination, fertility drugs, and in vitro fertilization. They have so much higher success rates than they've ever had.

Don't sit there and ignore your problems until it's too late to fix them. Get in there. Be proactive about your health! Also, if the doctor you choose ignores your concerns, find another! You're not stuck with just one doctor. If you think there's something wrong, go with your gut. I've found my gut is almost always right.

3. Don't forget to take care of yourself.

Don't be guilty of being so focused on creating a new life that you forget about you and the other sides of your health! Besides, these other health concerns are just as crucial to your reproductive health.

- *See Your Dentist*

When you're trying to conceive, be sure to consider your dental health. You see, you may not know this, but pregnancy hormones can actually cause gum disease if your mouth is cared for properly. Because your estrogen and progesterone levels will be higher, your gums will react differently to the bacteria that are housed in plaque. The bacteria will cause your gums to get red, swollen, and tender, and they'll bleed when you brush and floss. *Don't worry. It's perfectly normal!*

- *Ask for a Mental Evaluation*

Did you know that you're twice as likely to have infertility problems if you suffer from depression? Alice Domar, the director of the Domar Center for Mind/Body Health at Boston IVF, makes the suggestion that any woman trying to conceive, especially those with a family history of depression, do a mental health check. If you're clinically depressed, your psychiatrist can help you find a therapist and medication that will help. Your therapist can help you find information on stress management techniques, which is proven to further help depressed women in their journey toward conception.

- *Be Sure to Avoid Infections*

Certain infections can hurt your baby-to-be and even lead to miscarriage. Stay away from foods like cold deli meats, unpasteurized dairy products, unpasteurized soft cheeses, and raw and undercooked poultry and fish. These can cause listeriosis. Unpasteurized juices can carry E. coli and salmonella. Wash your hands so much they chap when you're making your food. No. Really, wash them often... very often. Your refrigerator should be set between 35 and 40 degrees Fahrenheit. Your freezer should be set at 0 degrees Fahrenheit or below. You should wear gloves when you're working in your garden in case the neighborhood cat used it as a litterbox or when you change the litter box so you don't get another infection called toxoplasmosis. It'll be quite unsafe for your baby when you conceive. Lastly, get the flu shot. The flu can lead to extreme illness during pregnancy, causing even preterm labor. I know you're not pregnant yet, but, when you're trying to get there, you never know when your egg *will* be fertilized and that baby of yours will cozy up to your uterus.

- *Don't forget about your spouse.*

Remember all the things we've been talking about that can harm your fertility—the alcohol, the cigarettes, the bad diet, being overweight, the unpasteurized soy, and so on? All those things that can do a number on *your* fertility… yeah, they can do a number on his too. They can cause low sperm count, lesser ability to swim (no swimmers, no babies), unhealthy sperm, and more.

He also needs all the nutrients we discussed—the vitamins, the minerals, the antioxidants, and the natural supplements. He needs to start with the proper diet, exercise, and healthy eating and vitamins the same time you do—three months before you begin stuffing those sheets. It will take him almost three months to make new sperm. He needs to be thinking ahead too *just. like. you.*

Increasing fertility doesn't have to be difficult. There are so many things you can do that will help you in this area. There are some vitamins, antioxidants, and natural supplements that'll help with this. Make sure to do the "do's" and avoid the "don't." And, remember, it doesn't *just* have to do with you. It has to do with you. It has to do with your spouse's health also. Get him involved. After all, the longer you have to wait to hold your baby, the longer he has to wait too.

CHAPTER FIVE: *TESTING TIMES!*

They say "the sooner, the better" for many things. The sooner you get your "chores" done, the sooner you can get to want to do. You should visit your family sooner than later. You never know what might happen. The sooner you train your pet, the sooner he'll be able to bring you joy rather than trouble and frustration. The same is true for testing for pregnancy. The sooner you know that you're pregnant, the sooner you can get into your OB/GYN or midwife to get prenatal care.

IT TAKES TIME

Although there are a few pregnancy tests that allow you to test as early as ten days after ovulation, you can get false negatives, where the test gives you a negative result when you're really pregnant too. This can delay prenatal care. You see, home pregnancy tests work by picking up on hCG, or human chorionic gonadotropin, on a pee stick. To test positive, they have to pick up 50 units of hCG. Testing early, even with a test marketed as "early response" or "early result," may simply not be picking up that level of hCG. You should really wait until the day your period is due to test. Waiting until then will give you the most accurate results.

TOO EARLY?

Everyone's different. Some women show a level of 50 units long before their period comes. Some women must test later than the day their period is due.

"What about those tests that *say* they show results early?" The truth is that, though they might, they don't always. The results of the tests that claim to show if you're pregnant *before* your period only work for those women whose hCG grows quickly. If you *are* planning to use an early response test, choose which one you want to use by checking the packaging to see how accurate each test is.

"How can I up my chances at a true reading?"

- Take the test upon waking. The hCG in your urine tends to be higher first thing in the morning.

- Follow the directions meticulously.

- Watch the expiration date closely. Don't use it if it's expired.

****NEGATIVE TESTS****

If you didn't get pregnant again this month, don't let yourself get upset. Maybe you've not been calculating your fertile days correctly. In that case, fertilization may have never had a chance to occur.

Do you remember the statistics I gave you in the last chapter on pregnancy? It takes 59% of women three months to conceive. Remember, only 30% conceive that first month.

Sometimes you can get what's called a "false negative." If you test negative, take a second test about a week after your period is due to start. If you're pregnant, your hCG level will double every 48 to 72 hours, so your test won't stay negative long.

The Wait

When your test is negative, it makes it really hard to hear how "lucky" so-and-so has been. This friend is pregnant today, and your cousin's friend got pregnant as of tomorrow. It can bring almost a pain to your heart—especially when you've been trying a while!

You know how our mind, as a woman, works. We worry all the time. "What if I can't get pregnant?" "What if I'm not doing it right?"

We worry about everything, don't we? "What if the van's new brakes are defective and it rolls down the hill overtop the neighbor's fence?!" I know my example seems silly, but we really are like that sometimes. We women are just downright nuts!

Just hang in there. Don't throw out your fertility chart just yet. Don't forget, some women take up to twelve months to get pregnant.

Test After Test

The emotional roller coaster of test after test can really get to you. After a while, you start to thinking you're pregnant every month, and, in all fairness, period symptoms and early pregnancy symptoms are very similar.

Period Symptoms	Pregnancy Symptoms
Tender breasts	Tender, swollen breasts

Bloating, fluid retention	**Bloating**
Abdominal Cramps	IV. Slight bleeding or cramping
Muscle aches	*
Headaches	V. Headaches
Acne	*
Diarrhea or constipation	VI. Constipation
Lower back pain	**Lower Back Pain**
Trouble sleeping or Low energy and fatigue	VII. Fatigue
VIII. *	IX. Nausea with or without vomiting
X. Cravings	XI. Food aversions or

	cravings
XII. Mood Swings	**XIII.** Mood swings
XIV. *	**XV.** Faintness and dizziness
XVI. Period	*XVII. Missed Period*
XVIII. *	**XIX.** Just "Feeling" Pregnant

Enduring the Wait

The two-week wait, riddled with high hopes, aspirations, and frustration, is the fourteen days between the day you ovulate and the day your period is supposed to hit. Those two weeks are riddled with the "what ifs" and the "am I"s. How do you make it those two weeks? Here are some survival tips for making the two-week wait more bearable.

- **Stop Overanalyzing Your "Symptoms."** Is that twinge in your pelvic area a sign of early pregnancy or just a simple twinge? Are you pregnant or simply catching that bug going around the office? Are you bloated only because of that broccoli you had last night? Many times, when "pregnancy symptoms" pop up, it's just symptoms caused by the normal hormones that come along after ovulation hits.

- **Don't Waste Your Time Searching Your Symptoms—** I'm the Google queen. I Google everything, and Google usually tells me my symptoms mean I have cancer and am going to die. If you google a symptom you're having and ask the internet if it's pregnancy or not, it'll tell you that you *might* be pregnant or you *might* be about to start your period. It might even tell you that you have GERD and esophageal cancer. Not only will these searches cost you hours of your time, but they'll make the two-week wait seem to take so much longer!

- **Keep yourself busy—your body and mind.** Remember the old adage that time flies when you're having fun? But what about when you're just sitting around doing nothing? Think about all those times when you sat in the office with time crawling by? Remember when you were ten and time seemed to move backward on Christmas Eve?

What about during that two-week wait? Don't sit around and stare at the clock then either! Get out there and do something. If all else fails, read a book or do sudoku, but do something.

**_Here are some ideas:_

- Go to the theater with some friends, or have a date with Redbox, your spouse, and a bag of popcorn.

- Clean. *Ha ha!* Just think of how much Spring cleaning you could get done if you kept yourself busy playing maid every four weeks for two weeks at a time! *Shhh! I don't suggest sharing this secret with your mother-in-law!*

- Hold an "un-procrastination day." Do all things you've *meant* to do and have just never gotten around to.

- Let your two-week wait mark the beginning of a beautiful thing—your taking up of a hobby or instrument you've meant to learn.

- **Just relax.** We've already talked about how relaxation techniques, like yoga or meditation, can improve fertility, but it can help you survive that two-week wait too!

- **Play therapist, doctoring *yourself*, of course.** Ask yourself your "what-if" questions and then answer them. If you find the root of your worry, maybe you can relax about that particular "what-if" at least!

Don't forget how important it is to act like you're pregnant when you're in the pre-pregnancy stage... especially when you're actively "trying." Faithfully take your prenatals. Stay far away from drugs. Avoid alcohol. Trash the cigarettes.

Doctors advocate moderate exercise during the two-week wait. Not only does it help pass time, but it helps with relaxation and lessens anxiety.

Why Does It Take So Long?

Don't forget your Biology courses—the birds and the bees. Pregnancy results due to several steps. In order to get pregnant:

- You must ovulate, which doesn't always happen.

- Your egg must then travel down your fallopian tubes and toward your uterus.

- During sex, your partner must ejaculate a healthy sperm.

- His sperm must travel into your uterus.

- The sperm must fertilize your egg, which means calculating your ovulation cycle correctly and more.

- Your egg, once fertilized, must implant in your uterus.

- The fertilized egg must stick.

So many things can go wrong. You can miscalculate your ovulation. Your cycle may run too short or too long. Your spouse might not have healthy sperm that month. You may not produce enough of the right hormones.

It may seem like it takes forever to conceive your bundle, but it seems so much longer if you find yourself with that question of "Why" on your lips. Everything must align perfectly for you to get pregnant. Don't forget that during the testing times. It's not a "Why", it's an "Oh!" You'll get it figured out. You'll learn your body. If conception just doesn't happen, you know when to visit the specialist. Don't give up. Keep trying. Keep testing.

Chapter Six: What If I Can't?

What happens if I can't pass my driving test? What If I can't walk down the aisle without tripping over my wedding dress? What if Momma gets in an accident on the way home?

Sometimes our worries are silly. Sometimes they're relevant, and sometimes they're necessary to pursue. Worrying if you can conceive can fall into all three.

It can be a silly kind of worry if you haven't even reached the "Stuffing the Sheets" stage or if you've just started it. Just keep trying. If you remember, it can take up to a year to get pregnant. However, if you've reached your year and surpassed it and still haven't conceived, it's time to start asking questions.

INFERTILITY

This word, infertility, is relevant to everyone—men and women alike. According to the Centers for Disease Control and Prevention (CDC), about 6.1 million American women have fertility problems.

Some have a hard time getting pregnant. Others have a hard time staying pregnant. Some of the types of infertility include:

- **Polycystic Ovarian Syndrome (PCOS)**—The most common cause of infertility, about five million American women have PCOS. Since women don't usually seek help for their symptoms until they have trouble conceiving, and because none of the symptoms ever seem related, less than 25% of those living with it have actually been diagnosed. Millions go undiagnosed.

Some of the signs of PCOS are having more male hormones than you should and less female hormones than you're supposed too. The common symptoms include irregular menstrual cycles, several ovarian cysts, fertility issues, acne, excessive facial and body hair, obesity, and depression. Everyone's symptoms may not present the same, as they differ from person to person. For example, though 80% of those with PCOS are obese, the other 20% show no signs of weight gain at all.

- **Endometriosis**—With this condition, your uterus lining is outside your uterus. About 6.5 million in America have it. About 40% of those have difficulty conceiving due to a blockage caused by adhesions or scarring.

- **Premature Ovarian Failure (POF)**—With this malady, your body would quit menstruating before you hit early menopausal age (which is 40 years old). POF can be caused by any number of things including chromosomal abnormalities created before birth, resulting in defective ovaries, your ovaries becoming hormone-resistant, chemotherapy, pelvic surgery, radiation, or just having it in your family history (*Don't worry too much. This is rare*).

POF also has as a sporadic side called intermittent ovarian failure. With this condition, you can have just a few periods a year... more or less... with months of having no menstruation at all. If you get tested for it while you're within a period of time that you're menstruating, the tests will show everything as normal.

- **Luteal Phase Defect (LPD)**—Two things cause LPD. These are (1) the inability of your ovaries to secrete enough progesterone, and (2) the failure of your endometrium to respond to the progesterone your ovaries do secrete. LPD will either bring with it fertility problems or result in an early miscarriage if it's left untreated. If you're diagnosed with LPD, you'll usually be prescribed hormones or stimulants of some sort. These will help your endometrium develop as it should so your pregnancy can progress.

- **Uterine Factors**—There are several causes of infertility that have to do with your uterus. Some of these problems might include uterine didelphys (when your uterus is divided by two walls), uterine fibroids, having scar tissue inside your uterus, not having a uterus at all, and more.

- There are several other causes of fertility problems that I haven't listed.

INFERTILITY AND MISCARRIAGE

Miscarriage (sometimes referred to as spontaneous abortion) is an unprompted loss of pregnancy from anywhere between conception to the gestational age of twenty weeks. It's very common according to the professor of obstetrics and gynecology and women's health at the Albert Einstein College of Medicine and Montefiore Medical Center in the Bronx, New York, and a medical adviser to the March of Dimes, Siobhan Dolan, MD, MPH. It's believed that about half of all fertilized eggs result in miscarriage before they're even known about, before they're able to implant. Ten to twenty percent of known pregnancies end in miscarriage. Having multiple miscarriages can be your first indication at fertility problems.

In 2005, my husband and I found out we were expecting our first baby. We were overwhelmed with joy and gratitude to God! We were going to have a baby!!!

When our baby was eight weeks, five days old (gestational age), we had a miscarriage... our first. It was devastating. So many people tried to help by saying things like, "You can always have another one," "Well, at least you were only 2 months along instead of 8 months", and "Think of all the people who can't have children... You're lucky that you can get pregnant!"

They WERE trying to help... but it didn't help. My heart was broken, my hopes were dashed, and my uterus, which had been carrying a baby... our baby... was empty.

What I really needed was time... time with God, time with my husband, time alone... time to heal. I needed to quit hearing people talk about my baby... my baby... as an IT. My baby was a living person... a very real, living person, not an IT. I needed to be loved, but I needed people to quit reminding me about my loss.

Yes, I know there are people... many people... who suffer from infertility. I know there are people whose arms ache to hold a precious bundle of joy of their own. I knew that then too but knowing that didn't help me at the time. [All I could think about was that I wanted my baby. Many women today feel the same way. They just want their baby...]

Harvey, Nishoni L. "Our Newest, Grandest News." Blog Post.* Becoming a Humble Home Homemaker. Blogger, 11 Sept. 2012. [USED WITH PERMISSION]

Some Causes

- Experts believe that most miscarriages come about due to genetic problems in the embryo, causing the baby to be unable to develop as he should. Some think these defects would have prevented him from being able to survive after birth. These miscarriages are usually not related to any kind of infertility problem or genetic problem in the mother.

- At other times, certain medical conditions or illnesses can increase your risk of, or cause, a miscarriage themselves. For instance, some viral infections can possibly spread to the placenta. Thyroid disease and diabetes are two other things that can cause significant complications.

265

Some Risks

There are other things can be a **risk** to pregnancy rather than a **cause of** miscarriage. Some of these are:

- A previous miscarriage

- Drinking alcohol (moderate to high intake)

- Smoking more than ten cigarettes a day

- The use of illicit drugs

- Using nonsteroidal anti-inflammatory drugs (NSAIDS) around the time you conceive

- Exposure to radiation

- Older maternal age

- Trauma caused to the uterus

- Uterine abnormalities

- Having a low or high BMI (Remember, these are *risks* NOT *causes*.)

Good News!

As devastating as miscarriage can be… especially when it involves with your first little miracle, there is some good news. It's not the end. One miscarriage, or even two, doesn't always mean infertility is on the table! In fact, most mothers who miscarry go on to have happy, healthy babies. I had two miscarriages. **Two.** And went on to have four healthy children!

Another word of "Yay"! Remember, there are treatments available for the many different types of infertility, even the many that result in miscarriage. However, if medications don't work for you, there are other methods for conception. They're explored further down in the chapter.

****IT MAY NOT BE YOU!****

Here's some more good news for you! It may not be a problem with *your* body! I know that doesn't solve the problem, but it does kind of make you sigh in relief, take a deep breath, and stand back and look at the situation in a whole new light. It may *not* be you.

Is infertility *just* a woman's problem? *NO!!* *Happy dance!* Both of us—men and women alike, can have fertility issues. In fact, about one-third of all of the infertility cases that have been presented before doctors have stemmed from men.

No, this does *not* mean two-thirds stems from women. Only one-third comes from our gender as well.

"So... um... Where'd the other one-third go?" *Glad you asked!* The remaining one-third of all the infertility cases presented are either caused by unknown problems or by a mixture of his problems and yours.

THE MALE FACTOR

I know it makes you feel better, but, in glorying in the pressure being taken off your shoulders, remember what he must be feeling like. Most men don't take "you can't"s very well. Being told they can't perform as they should in making babies is going to make them upset and anxious—whether they want to admit it or not.

Don't forget about him. Work through this together. Be there for him. Be his rock and be his pillar to lean on.

This is one thing that affects him so drastically still affects *both* of you. You're *still* a team. Get in there and be his cheerleader. There are ways to possibly fix this or to overcome it—just like there is with female infertility. Help him figure this out. Conquer it together!

Some Causes

- **Varicocele--**Sometimes the veins in a man's testicles can be too large, overheating them. This causes the shape and number of his sperm to be affected, causing infertility.

- **Blockage**—Some men have an obstruction at some place along their reproductive tract. The blockage could be caused by damage or any injury brought upon the reproductive system. This would keep their sperm from being able to follow its track.

- **Low Sperm Production**—Some men don't produce enough sperm or, even, any at all, which thwarts the sperm's ability to make it to the egg.

- **Sperm Shape**—The sperm's shape may affect its ability to move very quickly or, even, at all.

- **Failure to Ejaculate**—If your partner is unable to "shoot" sperm, you can't get pregnant. No sperm, no baby.

Some Risks

Just like the risks listed above in the woman's section—your section, these are *risks,* not *causes.* Don't confuse them for such. However, your spouse must remember that his sperm can be changed from healthy to unhealthy, or vice versa, by his lifestyle and overall health. Remember, we went over the fact earlier that a man's sperm is still affected nine months later by the choices he makes today. He should start avoiding the risks he can avoid nine months before you start stuffing the sheets. There are several things below that he'll have no control over. Some things that may lower your partner's sperm count or his sperm health are:

- Certain medications

- Smoking

- Drugs

- Alcohol

- Chemotherapy

- Radiation treatment

- Lead, pesticides, and other environmental toxins

- Age

- Serious health conditions, such as kidney disease

- Other health problems, such as the mumps

- Hormone problems

THE DOCTORS GET THEIR CUT

So, you're having trouble getting pregnant. You suspect fertility problems. How do the doctors get to the bottom of it? How will they even know if you're truly having fertility problems or not? What if you're just "having a hard time"?

There's a specific system they follow, though they follow it according to their own system and their own experience of what works best for *them* in *their* office. No two doctors may do it exactly the same.

First, they'll do an infertility checkup, which involves a number of things. They do a full physical exam and ask you and your partner about your sexual history and health—just like any doctor. Sometimes, a problem will come to light, but tests usually have to be run.

MALES AND FERTILITY TESTS

The testing for men starts out with a urologist and is almost as complicated as that which we have to go through. *Almost.* The tests your man will have to endure… up until something is found… will be:

1. **Sperm and Semen Analysis**—This is where most doctors start. Your partner's sperm will be analyzed by movement, shape, count, and other characteristics as well. Usually, the more normal sperm he has, the higher his fertility level. However, about 15% of those who are infertile test out as having normal semen and at least an adequate supply of normal sperm.

Sometimes, if the results to the first semen analysis test returns normal, a second test may be ordered to confirm the results. If there's anything that appears unusual, the urologist will order further testing to narrow down the issue.

If the analysis reveals no sperm at all, it may indicate a blockage in his reproductive tract. This can be fixed via surgery.

   2. **Immunobead Test**—This test is to check your partner's semen for anti-sperm antibodies. If your man's body makes the abnormal antibodies that some men's does, it may explain a lot. These antibodies attack the sperm as they try to swim toward your egg.

With an immunobead test, your partner will masturbate to provide the doctor with a semen sample that can then be tested. An alternative test would be the antiglobulin reaction test done on the blood.

** THIS TEST IS PERFORMED ON BOTH YOU AND YOUR SPOUSE IF IT BECOMES NECESSARY.

   3. **Urine Analysis**—With this test, the urologist will examine your partner's urine for semen before and after ejaculation. This test will only be performed if his semen and sperm count was very low or nonexistent. The doctor will be checking for retrograde ejaculation, which is when the sperm ejaculates backward, ending up in the bladder instead of on its way to

your egg. An earlier surgery on the penis is usually the cause of this condition.

4. **Cystoscopy**—This procedure is the insertion of a tiny tube, complete with light and camera, into the urinary tract to search the lower urinary tract for abnormalities. In this specific test, the urologist would be searching for the presence or absence of the "vas deferens" (which is *supposed* to be there). Some men are born without it. The vas deferens is the tube-like opening through which the sperm travels outside the penis when he ejaculates. If it's missing, there's no avenue for his sperm to get from his testes to your uterus.

5. **Genetic Testing**—As 10% of couples experience repeated pregnancy loss or infertility due to genetics (at least as a contributing factor), genetic tests can help doctors identify what specific problems your partner might have with his sperm or what fertility issues you or your partner might have. Taking a closer look at the DNA, via this testing, scientists can tell which gene changes you have that may cause you to have certain diseases or illnesses. This includes infertility.

6. **Hormone Evaluation**—A serum testosterone test checks your testosterone levels. Another hormone tested is FSH and, sometimes, LH, prolactin, or estradiol. Hormones control how

your body makes sperm. Doctors can't agree on how deep the search into hormonal causes for infertility should go since hormones seem to only be a problem in about 3% of all infertility cases.

FEMALES AND FERTILITY TESTS

Unlike our men, our testing begins in the OB/GYN's office. Other than the few tests above that are noted as available for both you and your spouse, some of the tests you will go through are:

1. **Charting**--The first step will be to check up on your body's ovulation habits. Your fertility specialist will have you track your ovulation. We've already covered this thoroughly so I won't spend much time here. Just as a refresher, you can track it yourself by (1) taking your daily basal temperature, (2) monitoring your cervical mucus, and (3) using home ovulation test kits.

2. **Ovulation Test Panel**—Your doctor can also check to see if you're ovulating correctly in his office via blood tests.

3. **Transvaginal Ultrasound**—Your doctor can also do an ultrasound of your ovaries. If it turns out that you're ovulating normally, it's time to move on to other testing.

4. **Laparoscopy**—This is a minor surgery similar to the cystoscopy used to check for your husband's vas deferens. During laparoscopy, your doctor will use a laparoscope, a small scope-like tool with a light on it, to explore your fallopian tubes, ovaries, and uterus for physical problems and disease. The reason it's considered a surgery, whereas a cystoscopy is a procedure, is because the laparoscope is inserted through a small incision the surgeon makes in your lower abdomen.

5. **Hysterosalpingography**—In this test, a special dye is injected into your uterus and fallopian tubes via the vagina. An x-ray of your fallopian tubes and uterus is then taken, and the special dye, which will show up on the x-ray, will move freely through the path the egg takes in its decent (and the path the sperm take in its ascent) if there are no blockages. Hysterosalpingography will reveal any physical blockages in "the system" that could be causing infertility.

Running all these tests can seem to take forever. It's a long and harrowing process. You don't need to worry if they don't find all the problems right away, but what if they don't find any problems at all? Does that mean there *are* no problems? No! One in every five couples is told there is no explanation for their infertility. In your case, there's merely no test yet developed that can identify the problems you're facing.

It is *not* "all in your head." There is no talking yourself out of the fact that you're infertile, and the most frustrating part of any diagnosis—especially infertility, is when they say they have no clue *what* is leading to that diagnosis.

Accepting your symptoms is easier, for some reason, when you know exactly what's causing them. This goes for infertility as well. One of the reasons it helps so much in infertility is that so much can be done to improve the infertile's chances at conceiving if the doctors know exactly what the problem is. What do you do when you have no clue? What are your options when everything is unexplainable?

Talk to your healthcare provider and your partner. You'll have to make a decision together. Keep trying? Keep hoping? Seek treatment? Start working toward adoption?

****TREATMENT OPTIONS****

There are several types of treatment out there. Medicine and surgery can both be used to treat infertility, which is usually the case. It can also be treated with assisted reproductive technology or artificial insemination, both of which we'll discuss later. There are many cases that a combination of these treatments is used. It often takes time and patience to find the right amount and combination of each to use in each case.

Your doctor will decide on which treatment to use based on several factors:

- How long you and your partner have been trying to get pregnant

- Your and your husband's overall health

- The test results

- Your and your partner's age

- Your and your spouse's preference

OPTIONS FOR MEN

Infertility in men is treated in different ways depending on the obstacle they face. A few of them are:

- **Low sperm count**—There are many reasons for a low sperm count, as we discussed. Some of these can be corrected through surgery. At other times, the fertility specialist can go in and directly remove your partner's sperm from his reproductive tract for use.

At times, there may be an infection that's causing a low sperm count or poor sperm health. These must be dealt with via antibiotics if the low sperm count is to be rectified. A few types of infections include epididymitis or orchitis. Other infections can also include some STIs like HIV and gonorrhea. There are also other infections, yet, that if left untreated, can cause permanent damage to your partner's testicles.

- **Impotence**—Fertility specialists can treat erectile dysfunction in any age group through drugs, surgeries, and/or devices. Some of the available medications include Levitra, Viagra, MUSE, and Trimix. Doctors also prescribe penile prosthesis, vacuum devices, and vascular surgery when necessary.

- **Blockage**—If anything is blocking your man's sperm from moving down through his system, microsurgery is, many times, the answer. Vasoepididymostomy is the method used to take care of obstructions, whether they be congenital, blockages caused from scarring (usually from infections), or whether the blockage is unexplained. If you and your partner choose to pursue this avenue of treatment, be sure to carefully select his surgeon. It requires substantial experience since it's one of the most difficult procedures in the microsurgical world.

- **Premature ejaculation**—The doctor will have counseling, behavioral techniques, oral medications, pelvic floor exercises, and topical anesthetics at his disposal to battle this. Topical anesthetics, applied ten to fifteen minutes prior to sexual intercourse will lessen the sensations, thus delaying ejaculation. Some of the medications doctors use to treat erectile dysfunction (phosphodiesterase-5 inhibitors), like Viagra, Levitra, and Cialis, may also help slow down premature ejaculation. Two other medications that help control premature ejaculation are analgesics (one of Tramadol's side effects is delayed ejaculation) and antidepressants (certain ones' side effects include delayed orgasm).

OPTIONS FOR WOMEN

There are several different medications that your fertility specialist could use to treat fertility problems. You must remember that every medicine has its side effects and possible dangers. Make sure to discuss the pros and cons with your doctor and spouse before pursuing medication.

Some medicines your doctor might use are:

- **Clomid (Clomiphene Citrate)**—This medication is usually used for those with ovulation problems, especially those with PCOS. Clomid acts as the pituitary gland, which helps your body ovulate.

- **Parlodel (Bromocriptine)**—Parlodel helps with ovulation problems caused by high levels of prolactin.

- **Repronex, Pergonal (Human menopausal gonadotropin or hMG)**—hMG helps women whose pituitary gland affects ovulation. It works by directly stimulating ovulation.

- **Gonal-F, Follistim (FSH)**—Working similar to the way hMG does, FSH starts up the process of ovulation. It's usually injected.

- **Glucophage (Metformin)**—Many fertility specialists use this drug in cases of women with PCOS and/or insulin resistance. Metformin will assist your body to lower the levels of male hormones in women with these physical conditions. There are times that this medication is combined with FSH or Clomid for better results.

- **Gonadotropin-releasing hormone (Gn-RH) analog**—If you don't ovulate regularly or tend to ovulate before your egg is developed enough to drop, doctors can use Gn-RH to "fix" your body. This medication acts on your pituitary gland, changing when your body ovulates. If you ovulate at the right time, pregnancy is definitely more possible.

**Several of the of the fertility drugs on the market may make your pregnancy higher risk by raising the chance of having multiples. Pregnancies involving multiples are more problematic. These problems include:

- Preeclampsia

- Intrauterine Growth Restriction

- Preterm Labor/ Delivery

- Cesarean

- low birth weight

- Fetal Demise/ Loss

ASSISTED REPRODUCTIVE TECHNOLOGY

Assisted reproductive technology (ART) is defined as any of the medical techniques used for helping infertile couples in boosting their fertility. Of all the births in America, about 1.7% are conceived via ART.

The success rates of ART depend on many things, such as the clinic, the type of ART used, how old you are, whether your egg is frozen or fresh, why you're infertile, and more. According to the Fertility Clinic Success Rates Report run by the Center for Disease Control and Prevention, of the 263,577 ART cycles performed in 2016, there were 76,930 babies born.

From that fateful night in 1965 when Dr. Robert Edwards, a physiologist at Cambridge University, combined a human ovum and his own semen in a petri dish, thus creating a human embryo to the day the first test tube baby was born on July 25th, 1978, ART has made leaps and bounds. Then, we make it to today, where there are several types of assisted reproductive technology available.

A.R.T.

- **Artificial Insemination (IUI)**—IUI is a procedure in which your partner's semen would be taken, specially prepared, and injected into your uterus at or during the time you would be due to ovulate. It may sometimes be necessary for your doctor to give you medications to push your body into ovulation.

Also known as intrauterine insemination, IUI is usually used by fertility specialists to treat (1) woman who have problems with their cervical mucus but have normal, healthy fallopian tubes; (2) men with mild factor infertility, such as the inability to erect; and, (3) couples that have unexplained infertility. It can also be used in the case of your partner's semen being frozen prior to cancer treatments or being frozen due to an extended absence.

- **Intracytoplasmic Sperm Injection (ICSI)**—ICSI is used to overcome male fertility problems caused by sperm issues. With ICSI, an egg is extracted from your ovaries, and a single sperm is injected in it. Your egg is then placed inside your uterus.

- **Donor Conception**—This includes donor eggs, sperm, and embryos.

Donor Sperm—Also known as donor insemination (DI), there are several areas it might be used:

- o When your partner doesn't have sperm that's normal;

- o When his body doesn't produce any sperm at all;

- o When he has a genetic abnormality or disease, or is a carrier, and has a high risk of passing it to the baby; or,

- o When you hope to get pregnant without involving a partner.

Donor insemination is completed the same way as artificial insemination is.

Donor Eggs—Some women donate their eggs to offer others who cannot produce eggs of their own a way to have their bundle of joy. Other reasons you or others might need to utilize this method of ART is:

- ○ If you have had recurrent miscarriages;

- ○ When your eggs are of low quality; or,

- ○ When you run the risk of passing on a genetic abnormality or genetic disease to your child.

For this procedure to be successful, the donor must take a hormone stimulant to produce multiple eggs. You may also be given hormones to prepare your body to accept your baby. Once the mature eggs are ready to descend, the fertility specialist will fertilize them with your spouse's sperm and let them incubate two to five days. After the healthy embryos have properly formed, one will be transferred into your uterus. You may also take hormones for about ten weeks after your baby has been inserted into your uterus.

Donor Embryos—Although it doesn't happen often, some people donate their unneeded embryos. These embryos would be available, having been left over from the donator's previous IVF and frozen for later use.

When you're ready to undergo donor conception, your doctor will
thaw out the new member of your family and transfer him to your
uterus, his new home for nine months.

- **In Vitro Fertilization (IVF)**—literally meaning "fertilized in the glass," as *in vitro* is Latin for "*in glass.*" IVF is a procedure in which you would be given a medication to prompt your ovaries to produce several eggs. Those few eggs, then, once mature, will be taken out of your ovaries and transferred to a dish in a lab—into a "glass." There, they'll be fertilized with your partner's sperm. Between three and five days later, the healthy embryo(s) will be implanted into your uterus. If several of your embryos develop, you can freeze them for later pregnancies if you want too!

IVF will be used if your spouse's body can't produce enough sperm or if there is a blockage in your fallopian tubes, not allowing your eggs to descend. At age thirty-five, the success rate is 47.5%. It is 39.6% from thirty-five to thirty-seven-years-old and 28% from thirty-eight to forty.

- **Zygote Intrafallopian Transfer (ZIFT)**—Though it has become less common since IVF has become so successful, ZIFT still has its place as a "more natural way" of ART. If you chose to use ZIFT, your eggs would be taken from your body and the sperm taken from your partner's. They would be placed together inside a lab, where they'd be mixed together rather than having the sperm injected into the egg. The fertilized eggs would then be inserted back into your fallopian tubes.

- **Surrogacy**—Couples must sometimes use surrogate mothers to carry their babies for them. If you don't have any eggs or if your eggs are too unhealthy to conceive a baby of your own, your baby can be conceived from your partner's sperm or a donor's sperm and the surrogate's egg. The surrogate, who agrees to donate her own egg, is the baby's gestational mother. She agrees to give your baby to you and your partner by adoption after birth.

- **Gestational Carrier**—If you're fertile but have had to have a partial hysterectomy or have no uterus for another reason, you can still have a baby that is bone of your bones and flesh of your flesh via a gestational carrier. The carrier, therefore, will not be related at all to your baby and has no rights to him at birth.

This is also an option for those of us, like me, who should not get pregnant due to health complications (I had Post-Partum Psychosis with my youngest and was told to not get pregnant again. My seizure disorder also makes my pregnancies a little more complicated).

POOR RESPONDER

If you've taken medication to stimulate your ovaries and have still not ovulated, you, my friend, are a "poor responder." You'll need a higher dosage of medication, and it still may not work. If you're considering IVF, you might want to think about having an ovarian reserve test done first. It will save you money, time, and stress. You see, it'll tell you if you're a good candidate for IVF or not. There are many women who cannot conceive through IVF when they find themselves unsuccessful through fertility drugs. If you *are* a good candidate, you may want to consult with your doctor about trying a variety of stimulant drugs to discover which you might be respondent to. If you do decide to keep pursuing treatment, you should do so through a facility that has experience with other "poor responders." If the facility you're getting care through knows "poor responders" well, they'll be able to better help you.

WARNING!

The CDC has performed some studies recently showing ART babies to be more susceptible to certain birth defects. They may be two to four times more likely to have defects like a cleft palate or cleft lips and digestive system or heart problems. It may be due to the increased age of the parents above the average age of birth parents? It may be due to the technology? It may be due to other factors? No one really knows right now. There needs to be more research. The risk *is* pretty low, but it's definitely something you and your partner will want to consider when you're thinking about using Assisted Reproductive Technology.

It is, however, an option—one you and your partner will have to explore together. Weigh the pros and cons, talk to your doctor. Consider talking to a counselor. Whatever you choose, make sure it's what you both want for sure before moving forward. Good luck and may your baby stick!